The Mysterious Matter of Mind

About the Author and Respondent

ARTHUR C. CUSTANCE

Arthur C. Custance holds a Ph.D. in anthropology and an M.A. in oriental languages. His Ph.D. work was primarily completed at the University of Toronto. His Ph.D. degree was granted at the University of Ottawa following a move to Ottawa to direct the Human Engineering Laboratories of Canada's Defense Research Board. During his years there, Dr. Custance also completed the university's course in medical physiology. His research centered on the problem of heat regulation in humans under stress. His reports on this research have been published in a number of scientific journals. Now retired to full-time writing, Dr. Custance is the author of a wide range of books including the ten-volume *Doorway Papers,* which covers a broad spectrum of correlations between science and Christian faith. Dr. Custance is a Member Emeritus of the Canadian Physiological Society and a Fellow of the Royal Anthropological Institute.

LEE EDWARD TRAVIS

Lee Edward Travis is a physiological psychologist and a pioneer in the field of speech pathology. His B.A., M.A., and Ph.D. are from the University of Iowa, where he became head of the Department of Psychology. Later at the University of Southern California he founded and directed the speech and hearing clinic, established the first laboratory in the United States to record brain waves, was Professor of Psychology and Speech, and later was Clinical Professor. In 1965 he established the Graduate School of Psychology at Fuller Theological Seminary, Pasadena, California, where he is now Dean Emeritus and Distinguished Professor. Dr. Travis is a Founding Fellow with Honors and past president of the American Speech and Hearing Association. He is a Diplomate in Clinical Psychology of the American Board of Examiners in Professional Psychology. His book *Speech Pathology,* published in 1930, was the first in its field. He is author or editor of five books and a prolific contributor to professional journals.

The Mysterious Matter of Mind

Arthur C. Custance

with a response by
Lee Edward Travis

ZONDERVAN PUBLISHING HOUSE
OF THE ZONDERVAN CORPORATION
GRAND RAPIDS, MICHIGAN 49506

PROBE MINISTRIES
INTERNATIONAL
RICHARDSON, TEXAS 75080

Second printing 1981

Library of Congress Cataloging in Publication Data

Custance, Arthur C.
The mysterious matter of mind.

(Christian free university curriculum)
Bibliography: p.
1. Intellect—Philosophy. 2. Intellect—Physiological aspects. 3. Mind and body. I. Travis, Lee Edward, 1896- II. Title. III. Series.
QP398.C87 128'.2 79-24753

ISBN 0-310-38011-1

Place of Printing *Printed in the United States of America*

Permissions

page 64 Figure 3 and excerpts throughout this book are from John C. Eccles and Karl R. Popper, *The Self and Its Brain,* Figure E1-1, p. 229 and excerpts pp. viii-560 (copyright © 1977 by the authors). Used by permission.

page 68 Figure 4 and excerpts throughout this book are from Wilder Penfield, *The Mystery of the Mind: A Critical Study of Consciousness and the Human Brain,* Figure 5, p. 25, and excerpts pp. xiii-114 (copyright © 1975 by Princeton University Press). Reprinted by permission.

page 69 Figure 5 in this book is from Wilder Penfield and Phanor Perot, "The Brain's Record of Auditory and Visual Experience: A Final Summary and Discussion," *Brain* 86 (IV): 1963, p. 655. Used by permission of Oxford University Press.

Excerpts throughout this book are from Charles Sherrington, *Man on His Nature,* pp. 65, 210, 251 (copyright © 1963 by Cambridge University Press). Reprinted by permission.

Design Cover design by Paul Lewis
Book design by Louise Bauer

What Is the Christian Free University Curriculum?

The Christian Free University Curriculum is a continuing series on course topics and current issues relevant to today's academic community. The authors and publishers of the Curriculum, while upholding the necessity of a clear separation of church and state *as institutions,* have designed the Curriculum to contribute to the academic process and to the preservation of true academic freedom in the realm of educational ideas.

The series has been developed in a scholarly, nonsectarian way for use as classroom collateral reading. Inherent in its preparation is a recognition of the goal of higher education to consider a breadth of viewpoints in the quest for truth, understanding, and values.

The Christian Free University Curriculum is published jointly by Zondervan Publishing House and Probe Ministries International. Probe Ministries is a nonprofit corporation organized to provide perspective on the relationship of the academic disciplines and historic Christianity. Probe members and associates are actively engaged in research and in lecturing with students and faculty in thousands of university classrooms throughout the United States and Canada.

Christian Free University books should be ordered from Zondervan Publishing House (in the United Kingdom from The Paternoster Press), but further information about Probe's materials and ministries may be obtained by writing to Probe Ministries International, Box 5012, Richardson, Texas 75080.

Contents

Illustrations

Book Abstract

One's view of the origin and nature of mind is of crucial importance, both for an assessment of human worth and in the formation of a truly healthy philosophy of life.

Carefully examining historical outlooks on mind and brain, the author reviews various explanations which have been offered for the ascendancy of the mechanistic approach. He then presents the experimental findings of recent research which have led some of the most renowned scientists in the field to conclude that mind is more than matter and more than a mere by-product of the brain.

Such a conclusion provides a basis for rejecting the view that man is "nothing but" a machine, without in any way minimizing how remarkable this machine is.

Note Regarding Terminology

We live in an age of specialization. Specialization is usually accompanied by an extension of knowledge; but it also entails a certain hindrance to communication due to the emergence of technical jargons which, while they become binding factors within any community of scholars, at the same time exclude those to whom the jargon is unfamiliar. Words that are commonly used (or misused)—such as mind, will, consciousness, intelligence—are given specialized meanings which then become intelligible only to those who are party to them.

At a scientific symposium, people adopt such jargons and employ them almost like a foreign language to the mystification of the outsider. Communication ceases to be general.

Another consequence of this is that when quotable statements are taken from authorities in different fields in order to contribute light on some common theme, the same words sometimes mean different things when used by different authors. This potential for misunderstanding seems virtually unavoidable when any attempt at synthesis is made.

To seek to obviate this difficulty by an extensive note on the meaning of each key term as it appears can only confuse the average reader by leading him to suppose that every authority whose words are quoted is thereafter using his terms in *this* sense and *only* in this sense, which can sometimes be a misleading assumption.

Lord Bertrand Russell wisely observed on one occasion: "To be perfectly intelligible one must be inaccurate; to be perfectly accurate one has to be almost unintelligible!" The best one can hope for in a small volume like this, which calls upon the witness of authorities in one discipline to shed light upon the subject matter of another discipline, is at least to communicate some generative ideas. We may by opening up new lines of thought contribute light to minds of greater precision who will thus be enabled to hit upon the exact truth.

I have therefore followed what I consider to be the rather sane advice of two of the authors from whom I have drawn some of the most vital ideas: Sir Karl R. Popper and Sir John C. Eccles. The former is a philosopher of science with an international reputation as a profoundly creative thinker, and the latter has been for many years one of the most renowned neurophysiologists in the English-speaking world and a Nobel Laureate.

In the preface to their joint work of recent date (1977), *The Self and Its Brain,* they wrote:

> We agree on the importance of a presentation that strives for clarity and simplicity. Words should be used well and carefully (we have certainly not everywhere succeeded in this); but their meaning should never, we think, become a topic of discussion or be permitted to dominate the discussion, as happens so often in contemporary philosophical writing. . . . What we are interested in is not the meaning of terms but the truth of (our) theories; and this truth is largely independent of the terminology used. . . . What *is* important is not to prejudge the issue by the terminology used.[1]

In the present volume the multidisciplinary sources of information which hopefully will appeal to readers with diverse backgrounds does not allow the giving of precise definitions. Such an attempt would be abortive in the eyes of experts in different areas of research who would inevitably disagree with them.

A few terms have been "explained" in circular fashion (as very brief footnotes)—i.e., merely by suggesting their opposites as used elsewhere. Beyond this, we have to cast the text upon the indulgence of the highly sophisticated reader in the hope that the more general reader will be as excited and as stimulated by the current trends in research in this important field as the writer has been.

The Mind/Brain Problem

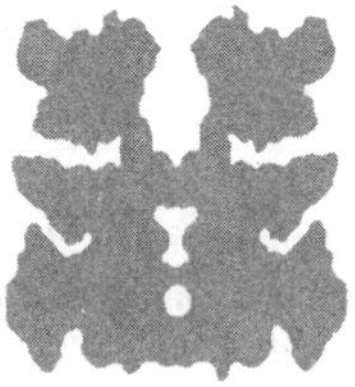

Chapter Abstract

The problem of distinguishing mind from brain and the historical concepts of the relationship between the two are reviewed.

chapter one

The Mind/Brain Problem

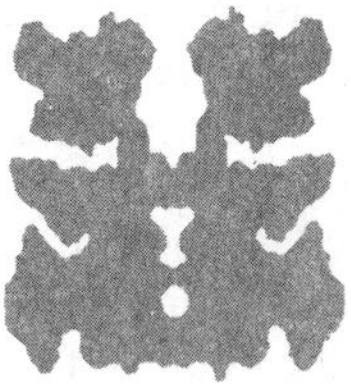

About forty years ago I was walking down Yonge Street in Toronto and ran into an old friend who had just retired after practicing medicine in Ontario and later in China for many years. He was clearly preoccupied. Over a cup of coffee, he shared with me an experience so moving that it had taken a weekend in the country for him to recover from it.

He had grown up in the Ontario countryside, a junior member of quite a large and very closely knit family on a farm. He had now retired to his homeland and was just strolling down Yonge Street, eyeing the old familiar sights and sounds when, suddenly and entirely unexpectedly, a lady wearing a perfume of a very special kind had passed him. The odor of it, when it reached his nostrils though only for a fleeting moment, instantly carried him back almost sixty years to an event in his early teens long since forgotten.

He found himself standing on the landing halfway up the winding stairs in the old homestead. It was almost suppertime. The table was being set in the dining room by his brothers and sisters with much noise of rattling dishes and silverware and laughter and hurrying steps. From the kitchen he could hear his mother as she prepared the meal, and the sound of wood being shoved into the stove and the stove lids and the pots and pans being moved about came back to him with unbelievable clarity. He wanted so badly to join in the fun but he had been made to stand on this landing with his face to the window because of some misdemeanor long since forgotten. The window was all frosted up and only the sounds and smells remained to stick in his memory, for he could not see anything outside. On the window sill was a pair of his mother's gloves, and from them there arose just the faintest odor of perfume—the same perfume that he had detected as he passed the unknown lady on his way down Yonge Street so many years later.

This small trigger to such a mind released what proved to be an emotionally overwhelming recall. Ushered suddenly into the nostalgic past, he had gone into the country for a few days to recover himself.

Consider what such an experience implies. The perfume, fleeting though its physical stimulus must have been, had somehow triggered his memory, switching on in his brain as it were a TV screen which he then seemed to be watching with his mind, enthralled by the vividness as the old familiar scene unfolded itself in great detail. *He* was not the screen but the viewer. And he appeared to be the *operator*, able to rerun the film and even slow it down and recover details missed on the first viewing.

It is as though some kind of self-conscious mind was using and manipulating a memory storage system that had preserved, for his later use upon demand, an extraordinarily vivid and complete record of a complex series of events occurring over half a century before it was again "called to mind."

When we met, he was in search of the lady—or more particularly the perfume—in the hope that he could experiment further and see what more might be recovered by means of the same trigger mechanism to recharge his power of recall.

Until recently, such an experience would have been

dismissed in scientific circles as purely anecdotal. The rigid controls demanded for scientific evidence, as well as the present climate of opinion regarding the relationship between mind and brain, have not permitted such evidence of dualism to carry any weight. Man has been held to be essentially an electrochemical machine. The self-conscious mind is not a *viewer* of the screen of the brain in the sense that this story implies. Mind is merely an extension of the mechanism of the brain and entirely dependent upon it. Such a view is by definition *monistic:* the brain acts upon the mind, which is a mere extension of itself, but the mind has no power to act upon the brain. The dualist, by contrast, takes the position that interaction is possible both ways, the mind acting upon the brain and the brain in certain ways limiting and channeling, and therefore acting upon the mind.

In this instance, one might argue that the mind was indeed an active independent agent, scanning the screened program which was stored in the brain. Furthermore, the subject himself experienced a strong desire to extend the retrieval and even fill out its detail. The "tape" was consciously and deliberately being replayed over and over again, with fresh content being added and sometimes corrected with each replay. The whiff of perfume was no longer needed to trigger the recall. The will or the self-conscious mind had taken control. How shall we evaluate the mind/brain relationship in a situation like this?

A Mind of Its Own

In 1961 Wilder Penfield reported a dramatic demonstration of the reality of active mind or will at work. He observed *mind* acting independently of the *brain* under controlled experimental conditions that were reproducible at will. His subject was an epileptic patient whose brain had been surgically exposed in the temporal area of one hemisphere. The "trigger" was stimulation of the cortex with a single electrode using a 60-cycle 2-volt current.

In a now famous paper, Penfield wrote:

When the neurosurgeon applies an electrode to the motor area of the patient's cerebral cortex causing the opposite hand to move, and when he asks the patient why he moved the hand, the response is: 'I didn't do it. You made me do it'. . . . It may be said that the patient thinks of himself as having an existence separate from his body.

Once when I warned a patient of my intention to stimulate the motor area of the cortex, and challenged him to keep his hand from moving when the electrode was applied, he seized it with the other hand and struggled to hold it still. Thus one hand, under the control of the right hemisphere driven by an electrode, and the other hand, which he controlled through the left hemisphere, were caused to struggle against each other. Behind the "brain action" of one hemisphere was the patient's mind. Behind the action of the other hemisphere was the electrode.

So he concluded:

There are, as you see, many demonstrable mechanisms (in the brain). They work for the purposes of the mind automatically when called upon. . . . But what agency is it that calls upon these mechanisms, choosing one rather than another? Is it another mechanism or is there in the mind something of different essence? To declare that these two are one does not make them so. But it does block the progress of research.[2]

It is clear that Penfield's epileptic subject had not only a brain capable of mechanistic manipulation but also a "mind of his own" by which the contralateral* area could be ordered to work at cross purposes. Here we are tempted to resort to a dualistic model, taking into account not merely a physical brain but some kind of independent and possibly nonphysical reality that interacts with the brain, and possibly *in* the brain, and yet not *of* it. But how can we account for "mind" if it did not originate in the physical world?

What precisely is the relationship between mind and brain? Is it merely a partnership of interaction? Did mind and brain evolve in independence and then run a parallel course of development? They might thus give a deceptive appearance of being causally related where causal relationship is in fact absent. Such a view would

---

*Contralateral—same *site* on opposite *side* (e.g., left eye is contralateral to right eye).

be termed *parallelism*. It is not strictly an explanation of the facts but more in the nature of a description of what could be happening.

Or was Berkeley right when he held that brain does not really exist, that the only reality is *mind* and that the concept of *brain*—indeed of the whole physical world—is a creation of thought, a product of mind, having no reality in its own right any more than a dream has. In one of the great Taoist classics, the book which is called *Chuang Tzu* (300 B.C. approximately) is said to be the work of a Chou dynasty sage named Chuang Chou. He appears to have been reminiscing when he wrote, speaking of himself in the third person:

> Long ago, Chuang Chou dreamed that he was a butterfly. He was elated as a butterfly—well pleased with himself, his aims satisfied. He knew nothing of Chou. But shortly he awoke and found himself to be Chou. He did not know whether as Chou he dreamed he was a butterfly, or whether as a butterfly he dreamed he was Chou.[3]

This approach to reality always involves ambiguity. Perhaps we shall all wake up one day and find an entirely different kind of reality. This is *idealism,* a not very satisfactory view—though certainly an intriguing one.

Or are the behaviorists correct when they say that only *brain* exists, and mind is just an epiphenomenon of it, as the electric current is produced by the generator? In this case mind has no independent existence and the question of the origin of mind is entirely secondary to the question of the origin and nature of brain tissue. This is *behaviorism*.

Behaviorism gained acceptance just after the turn of the century as the only possible view because scientific (objective) knowledge was held to be the only real knowledge man has. Scientific knowledge always depends upon measurables: it is quantifiable in one way or another. And who can quantify the mind?

Paul Weiss said,

> Maybe our concept of our nervous system is equally inadequate and insufficient, because so long as you use only electrical instruments, you get only electrical answers; if you use chemical detectors, you get chemical

answers; and if you determine numerical and geometrical values, you get numerical and geometrical answers. So perhaps we have not yet found the particular kind of instrument that tells us the next unknown.[4]

Obviously, we shall not even try to *invent* this particular kind of instrument of research so long as we accept the monistic view of mind as really only the outworking of brain. And certainly we are still bound by the older traditions of mechanism. Lord Adrian was reported not long ago to have observed, "The final aim of brain research must be to bring behavior within the framework of the physical sciences."[5]

This was a view (and an assured goal) of Claude Bernard, the progenitor of modern physiology. He held that the cause of all phenomena is matter, and determinism is "the foundation of all scientific progress and criticism."[6] Thomas Huxley reflected this position when he observed, "Thoughts are the expression of molecular changes in that matter of life which is the source of our other vital phenomena."[7] Again, "Mind is a function of matter, when that matter has attained a certain degree of organization."[8] And once again, "Thought is as much a function of matter as motion is."[9]

Such reductionism appeals to the mind that seeks for the simplest and strictly most quantitative picture of reality. Arthur O. Lovejoy, in his *Great Chain of Being*,[10] traces the history of the compelling search for connections throughout the natural order by which all things are derivatively related, a relationship which accounts for the supposedly linear progress from the simplest to the most complex. As "nature abhors a vacuum," so man abhors discontinuity. Ideally there should be no gaps, no missing links—in short, no novelties in the strict sense. A single start gives rise deterministically to all the branching realities, and every component in the evolving system must be accountable in terms of the rest and in no other terms.

This basic principle seems almost to compel assent in the thoughtful mind. In the natural order, each stage is merely an unfolding of the tendencies of prior stages. This is to be expected not only in the world of inanimate things but in the animate world as well. When understanding is complete, there will not be steps but only a smooth slide.

In the second half of the last century, three giants in the scientific world issued a *Manifesto*. These were Carl Ludwig (1816-1895), who taught most of the great physiologists of the world active in that age; Emil du-Bois-Reymand (1818-1896), who was the founder of electro-chemistry; and Hermann von Helmholtz (1812-1894), who needs no introduction. This, in substance, is what they agreed upon: "All the activities of living material, including consciousness, are ultimately to be explained in terms of physics and chemistry."[11] It is a kind of scientific ideal and still appeals with tremendous force to the modern scientific mind.

But while it may fulfill certain logical requirements to insist upon the monist view which makes consciousness a mere spin-off of the material body, it is for many people an unsatisfactory explanation of the phenomenon of *self*-consciousness. The problem is to find a way of treating mind and brain as a single phenomenon but yet as two realities. One answer is *identification theory*.

Identification theory has been known in two different forms. Both forms are expressed analogously—considered by many to be a weak argument which appears to explain more than it really does. Santayana and Thomas Huxley both proposed that as the noise of the babbling brook is only a by-product of the rushing water, so the mind, though distinct from the brain, is nevertheless only a by-product of it. The brain therefore causes the mind as the brook causes the babbling, but the mind cannot have any influence on the brain, any more than the babbling can have any influence on the brook. This was termed *epiphenomenalism*.

A more telling analogy is one which argues that as a single curved line has both a concave and a convex aspect, though the line is single and the two aspects are really one, so the brain and the mind are two aspects of a single phenomenon. The outer or physical event (brain activity) has an inner nonphysical aspect (mind activity). Neither causes the other, regardless of our impressions of their correspondence. Yet both must always occur together. This is known as *parallelism*, more specifically "double aspect" parallelism. The analogy breaks down, however, in that there can indeed be brain activity without mind activity, for brain waves are observable in the unconscious.

Cartesian Dualism: Mind and Brain Interaction

Chapter Abstract

René Descartes's view of dualistic interactionism is reviewed, and factors leading to its rejection are explored.

chapter two

Cartesian Dualism: Mind and Brain Interaction

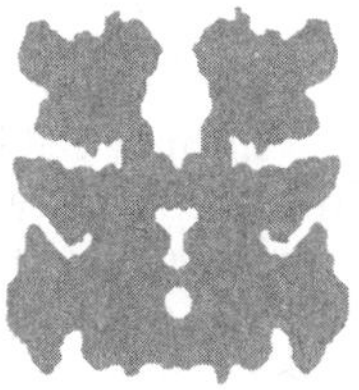

Dualism is an ancient concept and deeply rooted in Greek thought. The Greeks held that a man's soul was of an entirely different essence than his body. Furthermore, they held that these dual entities had no interaction with one another. Indeed, the Greeks saw them as alien to one another, the body being the prison house of the soul. Thus dualism means much more than a mere numerical designation. It implies the dichotomy of soul and body, an absolute split.

René Descartes (1596-1650) marks the beginning of *modern* psychology. He was a remarkable individual: primarily a philosopher, he was also a scientist, physiologist, and a mathematician.

He believed in an independent nonmaterial soul inhabiting and finding expression in a mechanically operated body. The reality of the body needed no proof, the reality of the soul did. Descartes used his famous aphorism as proof: *cogito ergo sum*, "I reflect, therefore I am." It is a neat form of proof and seems unanswerable. We cannot doubt the existence of our own self, because we cannot doubt it unless there is a self to do the doubting.

It is interesting that the idea did not originate with Descartes, though it is usually credited to him. Some twelve hundred years before Descartes, Augustine in his *City of God* (11. 26) wrote:

> Without any delusive representation of images and phantasms, I am most certain that I *am,* and that I know and delight in this. In respect of these truths, I am not afraid of the arguments of the Academicians, who say, "What if you are deceived?" For if *I* am deceived, I *am*. For he who is not, cannot be deceived; and if I am deceived, by this same token I *am*.

Descartes was concerned about how the nonmaterial could interact with the material and how the "extended" substance of body could house the "unextended" spirit called soul. He resolved the problem of the incompatibility of the two entities by his *dualism;* that is to say, by giving the problem a name.

He held that the two components which constitute man had an independent origin and are of a fundamentally different nature. The body could be divided up by the removal of a leg or an arm, but the soul was indivisible. The soul occupied the whole body in all its parts, but the reduction of the body in any way did not reduce the soul. The body was procreated, the soul was created. Though the two realities were of an entirely different nature, they could react upon each other, the soul on the body and the body on the soul. How this reaction takes place is a mystery nevertheless; only Descartes spelled it differently—*dualism*.

But he became the father of the mind/body theory of *interactionism*.

Descartes's Interactionism

Descartes held that the brain (along with the rest of the body) was purely mechanistic in its principle of operation. This is true when body is considered without soul—as he proposed was always the case in the animal world where soul is lacking. Thus animals are pure automatons. This mechanistic view of the body, including the brain, was not questionable if soul is not made any essential part of its operation. So Descartes was free to proceed with his physics of physiology.

But what then is the nature of the soul? His answer is simple: the sense perceptions and physical passions of men are dependent upon the body, but awareness of them lies in the soul. The important thing then is to enquire how the soul becomes aware (i.e., conscious and self-conscious) and how it succeeds in acting upon the body. Its awareness is due to the action of the body upon it, but how does it in turn act upon the body when it exercises will?

The point of interaction, according to Descartes, was at the site of the pineal gland, the only place he thought that is not duplicate as all other brain structures were thought to be. The soul was not, however, to be viewed as somehow shut up in the pineal gland. The gland is merely the point of interaction, not the seat of the soul in any fuller sense.

The body is extended matter: the soul is unextended spirit. When, however, the extended is acted upon by the unextended, some definite point of interaction is required and it is to be found in the pineal gland. Yet the "soul is united to all parts of the body conjointly." The whole body is the soul's proper housing so long as the body remains intact. When a member of the body—an arm or a leg, for example—is cut off, there is no loss of part of the soul as a consequence because the soul is unitary and indivisible. It then occupies what is left of the body.

So without attempting to resolve all the problems, he simply stated that there is a dualism of mind and body, and their interaction is clearly real. The brain is the major locus for the mind or consciousness of the soul, yet mind or consciousness is distributed throughout the whole body. The point of interaction between the two is the pineal gland.

Descartes lent his authority to the long-held view that the mind is associated in a particular way with the brain, but he made mind and brain separate entities, dependent upon each other only as a fountain pen and ink are interdependent. The pen will not write without the ink and the ink carries no message without the pen.

Descartes "substantialized" consciousness as unextended reality, something that can exist in the body but does not occupy space. Mind was real, yet entirely separate from matter and therefore from brain. *Interactionism* is his form of dualism. One extended and the other unextended, they nevertheless interact, and this interaction occurs at a specific site, the pineal gland. The theory cannot be disproved so long as there are mental phenomena whose neural correlates remain unknown. That there *are* mental phenomena cannot be doubted for reasons which are logically compulsive and were adopted (though not invented) by Descartes; they cannot be doubted because the very act of doubting them establishes their reality. The reality of conscious existence is confirmed each time it is denied.

Matter and mind he construed as created substances, each constituting a radically different and independent form of reality. Their interaction does not stem, he held, from a common origin. His inability to satisfy even his most ardent admirers on the nature of their interaction resulted in some of them adopting a view which came to be known as *occasionalism,* according to which each apparent interaction of mind and body was the result of direct divine intervention.

In the end, the Cartesian mechanistic view exempted only two phenomena from its all-embracing sweep, God and the soul of man. All else, all animal life below man and man himself save only for his soul, was encompassed in the universal chain of mechanistic causality. The concept was a grand one and ultimately proved too appealing to permit the one exception to be any hindrance to its application everywhere else. The soul was first ignored, then virtually denied, or made a mere outgrowth of the machine that was the body and the brain. In a lecture on Thomistic psychology given at the University of Ottawa in 1957, Professor R. H. Shevenell summed up Descartes's influence by saying:

> With Descartes, psychology lost its soul and found its mind: with British Empiricists, soul lost its mind and found its consciousness: with Watson and the Behaviourists, soul lost its consciousness and found its reflexes.

Descartes marked a turning point for the study of man, especially for the study of the mind/body relationship.

Most of the important thinkers who followed Descartes rejected interactionism. It was not a testable hypothesis. Above all, it introduced the supernatural into the picture and thus removed the concept from the scientific laboratory into the theological seminary.

Critics of his ideas objected that if soul and body were substances of entirely different natures, interaction between them was in fact impossible. This Descartes protested against, but he never satisfied his critics. Nor did *occasionalism* fare any better because interaction between mind and brain was now simply reduced to miracle, and miracles are not the domain of experimental science with its prime emphasis upon repeatability and quantification. It seemed the problem was insoluble and needed a new approach.

What emerged was a determination to reduce everything to physics and chemistry, or perhaps more precisely to physics and mathematics (though there are chemists who do not look kindly upon viewing their science as a branch of physics). But it must have encouraged Claude Bernard's approach to the body as a machine, and the success which attended this approach advanced our understanding of the body so remarkably that it became heresy to speak of dualism in the Cartesian sense.

But slowly, as the evidence has accumulated, it appears that the monistic* view is showing signs of insufficiency and a new dualism is in the making.

*Monistic: the opposite of dualistic, dichotomous, hyphenate.

Whence Came Mindedness?

Chapter Abstract

Animal and human consciousness are viewed in a continuum to seek an explanation for the mind's origin. Did mind appear "from nowhere" as a kind of direct creation, or was it always (but imperceptibly) resident in living systems?

chapter three

Whence Came Mindedness?

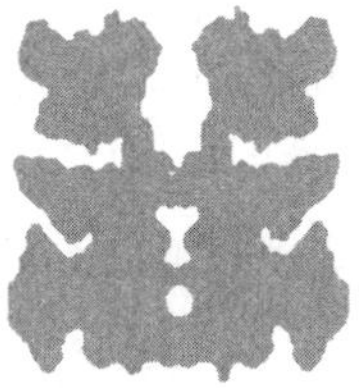

That we have something we call self-consciousness we cannot doubt even if we find it difficult to define precisely. J. R. Smythies (Department of Psychiatry, University of Edinburgh) wrote in 1969: "The consciousness of other people may be for me an abstraction, but my own consciousness is for me a reality."[12] That animals below man have consciousness seems clear enough. That they have self-consciousness is not so clear, in spite of the recent experiments in teaching the larger primates some form of sign language.

Further experiments with a chimpanzee have revealed that it was able to identify itself in a mirror as indicated by self-directed behavior. This is taken by some to demonstrate the possession of self-consciousness. But it may be necessary to distinguish between the self-consciousness of man by which he is aware of his own *mental* experience and the self-consciousness of an animal by which it is aware of its own *body*. The former seems clearly different from the latter.

The San Francisco *Chronicle* (21 July 1968) reported the case of a chimpanzee in the Chessington Zoo in England which, having been for years a show-off and fun-loving friend of the public, suddenly became shy and morose and took to hiding all day. The keeper decided that it was embarrassed because the hair on its head was thinning! It was provided with a toupee and this seemed to restore its "self-confidence" completely. But, again, one must ask, Is this kind of *body*-awareness to be equated with the *mind*-awareness that permits a person not only to think, but to think about his own thinking?

Zoologist W. H. Thorpe (Cambridge), a recognized authority in this area, wrote in 1974: "Sir Karl Popper agrees, I think, with most students of animal communication that consciousness of selfhood, that is, a fully self-reflective consciousness, is absent in animals."[13]

David Bidney (of the Graduate School, Indiana University) opens his study of *Theoretical Anthropology* with the following:

> Man is a self-reflecting animal in that he alone has the ability to objectify himself, to stand apart from himself, as it were, and to consider the kind of being he is and what it is that he wants to do and to become. Other animals may be conscious of their affects and the objects they perceive; man alone is capable of reflection, of self-consciousness, of thinking of himself as an object.[14]

Whether animals do have *self*-consciousness or not, there is at least no doubt that both animals and man have consciousness. Thus, even if we limit ourselves to consciousness as opposed to self-consciousness, we still have to ask, How did *it* arise?

Stanley Cobb suggests that "consciousness is an attribute of mind, that part which has to do with awareness of self and environment. It varies in degree from moment to moment in man, and from fish to man in phylogeny. It may be that invertebrates and even plants have rudimentary forms of awareness of self."[15] This sounds absurd. But if consciousness evolved from nonconsciousness, we should find, as we trace its development back to the properties of matter alone, that it becomes less and less manifest until it no longer appears to exist: or, in reverse, we should trace the development of matter until evidence of mindedness first emerges and is manifest. Such a manifestation would be a "new thing" (a *de novo*) but not a creation (*ex nihilo*) because it arises out of what already exists and without discontinuity.

It is important to distinguish a "novelty," which arises suddenly but has its origin within an existing system, from a "new thing" which has been introduced from outside the system. The first is something *de novo*, the latter is something *ex nihilo*. Since science cannot deal successfully with the latter, the idea of outright creation is not allowable. Within the framework of scientific thinking an object which is claimed to be *ex nihilo* is suspect, and a determined effort will be made to show how it can be derived from what already exists, however complex and novel it may appear to be. If mind arises *de novo* as an entirely new thing in nature, perhaps as the result of a mutation of some kind, it is nevertheless assumed that it is to be derived directly from what is already in existence. The idea of something new which has appeared *ex nihilo*, that is to say, *out of nothing*, is most unwelcome in the present climate of scientific thought.

We therefore have two basic views about the origin of mindedness, one of which is acceptable in spite of the mystery surrounding it, because it is derived out of existing matter. This is termed *monism*. The other view, which sees it as a direct creation, not derived out of existing matter but "out of nothing," is termed *dualism*. It is not scientifically respectable.

We may, however, make a further division of the subject by recognizing that within the strictly monistic view mindedness might arise *de novo* in two different ways. It might arise by slow emergence until it suddenly becomes recognizable as mindedness. Or it might appear by a single leap as soon as the complexity of the brain had reached a certain critical stage. The first is a gradual formation of a mindedness that was "always there" but at such a low level as not to be recognizable. This is the position of *panpsychism*, which holds that all matter has mindedness. The second is a sudden appearance of mindedness which thereafter has an existence in its own right, but born of existing matter nevertheless.

Dualism can also be conceived as occurring in two ways. Mindedness may be introduced *ex nihilo* in a kind of embryonic form which does not reveal itself until a certain stage of organic development has been reached. Or it is introduced *ex nihilo* only when this advanced stage of development has been completed.

Thus, although we have four alternatives, they can be viewed as two: monism and dualism. We may thus say that mindedness arose because matter contained within itself the potential for it; *or* we may say that it was introduced by some means external to matter. Either view presents a dilemma which has been recognized for a long time. In one case we must say that even atoms have potential mindedness—a circumstance which is difficult to conceive. Or we have the direct creation of something out of nothing—which is equally difficult to conceive. We face a hard choice.

The Case for Monism: Was Mind Always There?

In 1964 Cyril Ponnamperuma wrote a paper on "Chemical Evolution and the Origin of Life" in which he argued that "life is only a special and complicated property of matter, and that *au fond* (basically) there is no difference between a living organism and lifeless matter. . . ."[16] This implies that consciousness, which emerged out of living matter, must therefore also have been *latent* in nonliving matter.

This sparked some interesting correspondence in subsequent issues of the journal which had a bearing on the point. One of the correspondents, D. F. Lawden (University of Canterbury, New Zealand) remarked:

> If consciousness is a characteristic of this material aggregate (the brain), then by the principle of continuity it must also be a feature of every aggregate and ultimately of the fundamental particles. If this were not the case, at some level in the hierarchy* mentioned earlier, consciousness would arise discontinuously and it would be possible to draw a sharp dividing line separating conscious from non-conscious forms of matter. This would only be a disguised form of the line earlier assumed to separate

*i.e., "from inorganic, to organic, to biological chemistry."

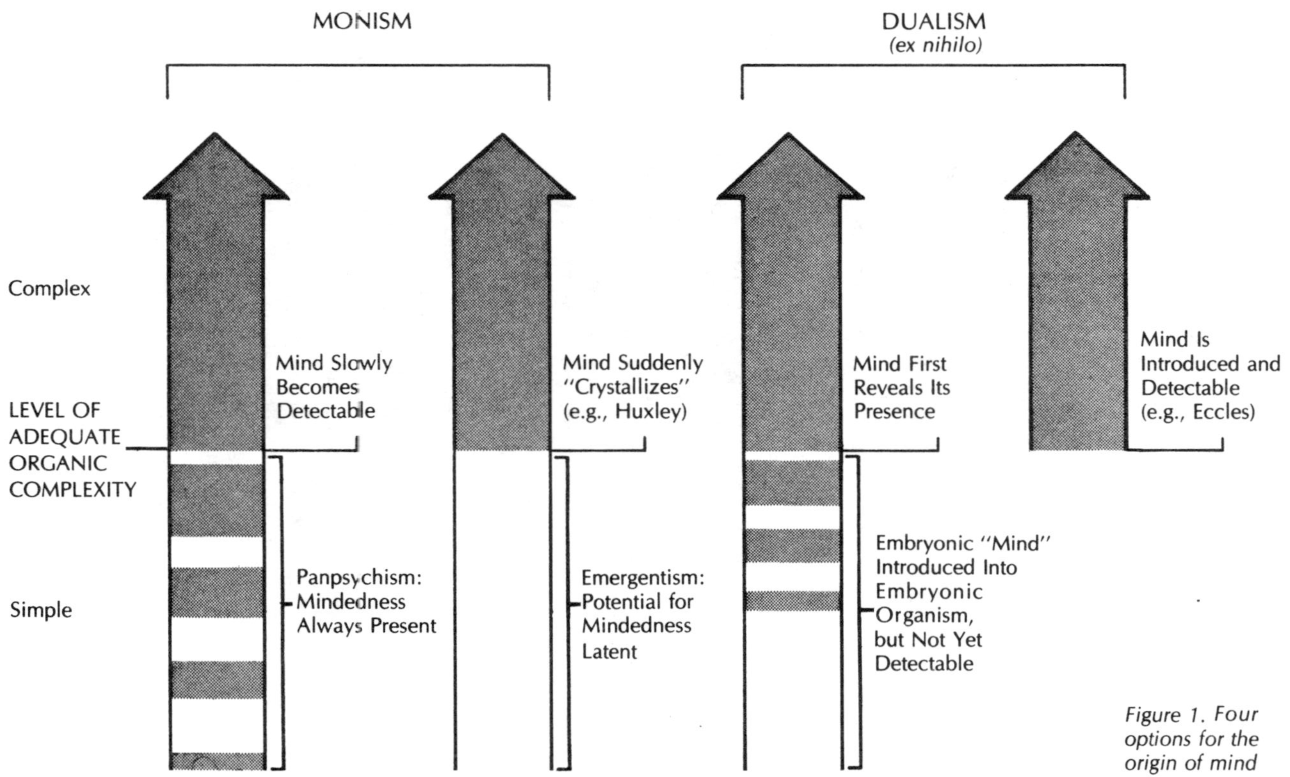

Figure 1. Four options for the origin of mind

living from non-living forms. Undoubtedly, such mental characteristics as are possessed by the fundamental particles must be of poor quality and weak intensity, but unless some such features are postulated, I fail to understand how consciousness could ever arise in any system of matter, however complex.

A system of particles, each of which possesses the known physical characteristics of electric charge, spin, etc., might very well be designed to behave like a human being, but not to *experience* consciousness as human beings undoubtedly do. . . . We may perhaps hope to explain human behavior, but our *experience* of this behaviour will remain unaccounted for.[17] (emphasis mine)

There, then, is the problem: our "mindedness" of our own behavior. . . . Where and how did it arise? Was "mind" introduced as something entirely new, or did it emerge simply because matter had reached the appropriate level of organization and had the appropriate capacities?

Furthermore, when we speak of reaching the appropriate level of organization, what precisely does this involve? Do carbon atoms have mindedness, either real or latent? How much organization of organic chemicals is necessary to support mindedness? There is evidence that some of the very simplest organisms display its presence.

H. S. Jennings long ago (1915) established the reality of "mindedness" in unicellular organisms. So clearly did he perceive this mindedness in amoebae, for example, that he had no hesitation in describing them as exhibiting *attention, desire, frustration, established habits,* and even *intelligence.* He wrote:

Intelligence is commonly held to consist essentially in the modification of behaviour in accordance with experience. If an organism reacts in a certain way under certain conditions, and continues this reaction no matter how disastrous the effects, we say that its behaviour is unintelligent. If on the other hand, it modifies its behaviour in such a way as to make it more adequate, we consider the behaviour to this extent intelligent. It is the "correlation of experiences and actions" that constitute, as Hobbhouse (1901) has put it, "the precise work of intelligence." It appears clear that we find the beginnings of such adaptive changes of behaviour even in the Protozoa.[18]

So, as far as the objective evidence goes, Jennings would hold to "a complete continuity between the ['minded'] behaviour of lower and higher organisms" in this respect.[19] He concluded:

> The writer is thoroughly convinced after long study of the behaviour of the amoeba, that if it were a large animal, so as to come within the everyday experience of human beings, its behaviour would at once call forth the attribution to it of states of pleasure and pain, of hunger, desire, and the like, on precisely the same basis as we attribute these things to a dog.[20]

J. Boyd Best found exactly the same wide range of minded responses in experiments with planarian worms, and concluded:

> One finds that planarian behaviour *resembles* behaviour that in higher animals one calls boredom, interest, conflict, decision, frustration, rebellion, anxiety, learning and cognitive awareness. . . . All one knows of the "mind" of another organism is inferred from its behaviour and its similarity to one's own. . . .
>
> If the major psychological patterns are not unique to the vertebrate brain but can be produced even by such primitive animals as planarians, two possibilities suggest themselves. Such patterns may stem from some primordial properties of living matter, arising from some cellular or subcellular level of organization rather than nerve circuitry. . . .
>
> An alternative is that behavioural programs may have arisen independently in various species by a kind of convergent evolution.[21]

We are thus led to the conclusion that even the *material* substance of the single-celled animal already has a kind of embryonic mindedness. Does all matter therefore have some kind of mindedness?

Arthur O. Lovejoy, in his *Great Chain of Being*,[22] observed that one of the principal motives of panpsychism is the desire to avoid any kind of real discontinuity, the independent introduction of any new thing into matter as soon as it has reached a certain level of organization capable of supporting it. This can apply equally to life or to mindedness. He pointed out that the French philosopher, J.-B.-R. Robinet, in his magnum opus *De La Nature* (published from 1761-1768),[23] argued that we must either attribute some appropriate form of consciousness even to stones, some level of intelligence even "to the least atom of matter," or we ought to deny the reality of consciousness altogether.

Twenty-five years ago, Sir Julian Huxley, driven by this kind of logic, observed:

> It would have been more correct to speak of the possibilities inherent in the world-stuff* (than in matter, per se); for the most startling potentiality revealed by the evolution is mind, and mind cannot be said to be contained, even as a potentiality, in matter. In most organisms—all plants, and all animal types produced in the early stages of evolution—there is no direct evidence of mind at work, no need to postulate mental properties. But higher animals are clearly the seat of mental processes akin to ours, processes of perception, cognition, emotion, will, and even insight.
>
> We must conclude that the world-stuff possesses not only material properties, but rudimentary potentialities of mental properties as well, and that these properties, when specialized out of their latent state into actuality, are of advantage to their possessors. . . .
>
> In most processes, the mind-aspects of the world-stuff are still as undetectable as were the electrical aspects of material processes up to the late nineteenth century.[24]

So the problem of the origin of mind now descends to the stuff of the molecules themselves. That molecules could carry some form of embryonic mind seems absurd, but it is necessary to assume some such potential unless we are to agree that mindedness arises *ex nihilo*. Indeed, this situation appears even in the developing embryo. That molecules do have some kind of protomindedness has been seriously proposed in recent years by a number of writers, among whom may be listed A. N. Whitehead, C. Hartshorn, Bernard Rensch, and L. C. Birch. These writers—Whitehead and Rensch in particular—ascribe some rudimentary

*By "world-stuff" Huxley does not seem to mean matter in some even more elemental form, but energy of some kind—though not personal energy such as a divine immanence.

form of life, sensation, and even volition to entities such as molecules, atoms, and subatomic particles.[25] One of Dobzhansky's senior colleagues, E. W. Sinnott, with whom he disagreed (though amicably), wrote a volume entitled *Cell and Psyche: The Biology of Purpose*. In this Sinnott remarked

> that biological organization [concerned with organic development and physiological activity] and psychical activity [concerned with behaviour and leading to mind] are *fundamentally the same thing*. To talk about "mind" in a bean plant . . . is more defensible than trying to place an arbitrary point on the evolutionary scale where mind, in some mysterious manner, made its appearance.[26] (emphasis his)

Logically he seems to be quite correct. It *is* logical enough if mind emerges automatically from brain at some stage in the elaboration of matter. But Dobzhansky held that this is "a kind of vitalism made to stand on its head."[27] Perhaps it is. However, it seems that if mindedness did not emerge automatically from brain, we ought to be able to locate the precise moment of its emergence. What would location of the precise moment of this emergent mindedness signify if there were no discoverable antecedents? A creation?

It would seem seem that Dobzhansky was prepared to allow that *life* would emerge automatically as soon as matter reached an appropriate stage of organization, and that consciousness would arise automatically, in its turn, when life reached a certain stage of complexity. What he was not prepared to agree to was that this matter was already in some sense alive, or that this life was already in some sense conscious of itself. There was no force acting upon dead matter to introduce life; it was only necessary that matter by chance reached the necessary stage of organization. And there was no necessity for some external force to act upon life to make it conscious of itself; it only required that life should have arisen to some higher level in order to become conscious automatically. What he objected to was the "always there" concept. Mindedness is seen as a new phenomenon, but it is not something introduced from outside, a creation *ex nihilo*, which had to wait until matter could provide a proper vehicle for it.

In another paper Dobzhansky restated his assessment of this "always there" position:

> Non-living matter, down to atoms and electrons, supposedly partakes of vital and volitional powers. In his imposing philosophical system, Whitehead has developed this view in some detail. . . . I must say that in my opinion [such] views must be rejected both on scientific and philosophical grounds.[28]

Yet on logical grounds one seems indeed to be on the horns of a dilemma. Just as in the case of life itself, either consciousness arose because the raw materials have the potential to give rise to it, or it arose *ex nihilo* from outside the system.

C. H. Waddington (of Edinburgh), reviewing Rensch's work *Evolution Above the Species Level* (1959), notes that the author

> finds himself driven to attribute a capacity for sensation to the lowest organized creatures which can be shown to be capable of learning, that is, coelenterates and possibly even protozoa. He seems, in fact, to agree in general with the outlook of A. N. Whitehead (to whom he does not refer) that something which belongs within the same realm of being as consciousness *has to be* attributed to all existing things, including the inanimate.[29] (emphasis mine)

It was the same logical compulsion that drove Sir Charles Sherrington to write:

> I would think that since mind appears in the developing soma, this amounts to showing that it is potential in the ovum (and sperm) from which the soma sprang. The appearance of recognizable mind in the soma would then be not a creation de novo but a development of mind from *unrecognizable into recognizable*.[30] (emphasis mine)

By this logic we come to the position of Whitehead and Rensch. One then has to ask, What was the form of this protomindedness that it could be potentially resident not only in the basic subatomic particles but even in these *particles* at a time when they were existing at the enormously high temperatures of their initial state as first brought into being? Somewhere one has to call a halt and say, "Here is where protomind began to exist." But where then did it come from to make that beginning even in its proto form?

When the Mindedness of Individual Cells Becomes a Shared Mindedness of the Multicellular Organism

Once mindedness or consciousness has appeared on the scene in unicellular animals, does the rest follow *automatically?* When single-celled organisms unite to form multicellular aggregates, does the protomindedness of the amoeba become the corporate mindedness of the larger mass? Is Lovejoy's "great chain" still unbroken?

Sherrington identified this problem in the developing embryo:

> The embryo, even when its cells are but two or three is a self-centered co-operating society—an organized family of cells with corporate individuality. . . .
>
> The human individual is an organized family of cells, a family so organized as to have not merely corporate unity but a corporate personality. . . . Yet each of its constituent cells is alive, centred in itself, managing itself, feeding and breathing for itself, separately born and destined separately to die.[31]

Evidently this aggregate or society achieves a sense of unification and the billions of selves becomes a single Self. Edward McCrady wrote some time ago:

> I, for instance, certainly have a stream of consciousness which I, as a whole, experience; and yet I include within myself millions of white blood cells which give impressive evidence of experiencing their own individual streams of consciousness of which I am not directly aware. It is both entertaining and instructive to watch living leucocytes crawling about within the transparent tissues of a living tadpole's tail. They give every indication of choosing their paths, experiencing uncertainty, making decisions, changing their minds, feeling contacts, etc., that we observe in larger individuals. . . .
>
> So I feel compelled to accept the conclusion that I am a community of individuals who have somehow become integrated into a higher order of individuality endowed with a higher order of mind which somehow coordinates and harmonizes the activities of the lesser individuals within me.[32]

How is this unification achieved? Most would say that it somehow does it itself. Sir Alister Hardy believes it is the result of some kind of group-mind, a mental telepathy at a very basic and semi- or subconscious level. He wrote:

> It is possible to imagine some such pattern of shared unconscious experience: a kind of composite species pattern of life. It is important to remember that in the concept of the individual mind we are faced with a mystery no less remarkable. The mind cannot be anchored to this or that group of cells that make up the brain. The community of cells making up the body has a mind beyond the individual cells—the ''impression'' coming from one part of the brain receiving sensory impulses from one eye and that from another part of the brain from the other eye are merged together in the mind (i.e., as a whole), not in some particular cells as far as we know.[33]

Lewis Thomas has a beautiful discussion of this gathering together to a critical size of the number of minded components that then make a fully conscious and purposeful whole.

> Termites are even more extraordinary in the way they seem to accumulate intelligence as they gather together. Two or three termites in a chamber will begin to pick up pellets and move them from place to place, but nothing comes of it; nothing is built. As more join in, they seem to reach a critical mass, a quorum, and the thinking begins. They place pellets atop pellets, then throw up columns and beautiful, curving, symmetrical arches, and the crystalline architecture of vaulted chambers is created. It is not known how they communicate with each other, how the chains of termites building one column know when to turn toward the crew of the adjacent column, or how, when the time comes, they manage the flawless joining of the arches. The stimuli that set them off at the outset, building collectively instead of shifting things about, may be pheromones* released when they reach committee size. They react as if alarmed. They become agitated, excited, and then they begin working like artists.[34]

Even more closely knit in organization is the conglomerate of free living cells which constitutes the Portuguese Man-of-War. This organism is really a

*A scent given off by one animal to signal to another.

colony of originally identical polyps, each of which is specialized for a particular function. But who or what decides which shall become the tentacles, or the floats, or the reproductive organs? And this Man-of-War is by no means alone in this respect.

Recent experiments have shown that healthy organs that have been teased apart will reassemble and show themselves to be, within the limitations of their isolated condition, functional. It has been demonstrated for frogs' eggs,[35] brain cells,[36] heart cells,[37] and kidney tissue.[38] It has even been reported that cells which prove to be deficient in some way in the reassembly process will be helped along if necessary by healthy cells.[39] Such a system of communication and coordination of activity suggests an organizing force or "field" of some kind (these words being used not because they explain anything but because they appear to cover our ignorance of what is going on).

So we see the possibility of mindedness in an individualistic form in the very lowest orders of life, and we see individualistic mindedness elaborated in conglomerates of cells which are able to communicate and constitute themselves into a larger form of mindedness. Nevertheless, the basic problem of whence arose mindedness, even in the unicellular forms, still remains behind all the later complications. We thus have the three possible views (see Figure 1): the panpsychic or "always there" view, the "sudden emergence" view, and the introduction of mind by creation *ex nihilo* view (with its two forms).

We have already referred to a remarkable volume written jointly by Sir Karl Popper and Sir John Eccles. Together they have examined, somewhat in the form of a debate, both the origin of mindedness and the nature of the interaction between mind and brain.

Both men reject panpsychism and agree that man ends up constitutionally as a duality of mind and matter, each of which has a measure of real independence and each of which interacts with the other.

Popper argues against the necessity of assuming that mind has been "always there" in matter. "We do not need to postulate," he says, "that the food which the body eats (and which in the end may form its brain) has qualities which can be, with informative success, described as pre-mental or as in any way even distantly similar to mind.''[40] All that is required is that matter has the capability of assuming a form that is appropriate to mindedness and that when this occurs, mindedness somehow appears.

Eccles holds that mind cannot be introduced until matter is sufficiently organized. But he argues that the organization of the individual as a unitary self out of the materials of the body is due to the self-conscious mind which neither is in the materials themselves nor arises out of them but is introduced from outside. The minded self is an active organizer that brings about unification and employs this unified system for its own purposes.

Both men are therefore dualists, though they hold differing views as to the *origin* of the mind. For Popper, matter *somehow* gives birth to mind; this is all that can be said about it. For Eccles, the origin of the mind seems more like a creation *ex nihilo* for each individual.

Before exploring their conclusions more fully, we turn to the experimental evidence that led them to accept an interactionist model.

A Theory Too Small

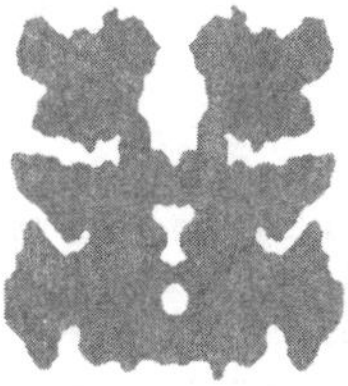

Chapter Abstract

A survey of dualistic thinking in the twentieth century, with special reference to the work and thought of Charles Sherrington, the father of modern understanding of brain function. The development of the mechanistic approach from a methodology to a pervasive outlook on all of life is traced.

chapter four

A Theory Too Small

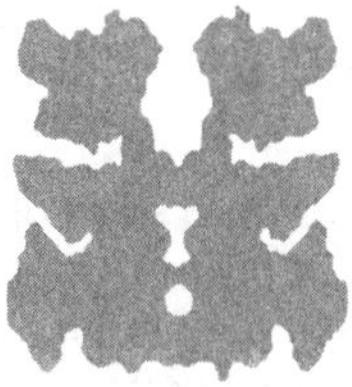

> The death on March 4, 1952, of Sir Charles Sherrington at the age of 94 marked the passing of the man of genius who laid the foundations of our knowledge of the functioning of the brain and spinal cord. His classic work *Integrative Action of the Nervous System,* published in 1906, is still a source of inspiration to physiologists all over the world. It was reprinted as recently as 1947 for the first post-war (World War II) International Congress on Physiology. His work did for neurology what the atomic theory did for chemistry. It is still as refreshing as it was in 1906, and it has needed no revision.

So reads part of the obituary notice in *The British Medical Journal* for March 15, 1952. And in a sense it sums up the originality and the quality of the research of a lifetime. Sherrington did not retire from the Chair of Physiology at Oxford until 1935 at the age of seventy-eight. Shortly thereafter he was invited to deliver the Gifford Lectures on Natural Theology at Edinburgh University (1937-1938), which were later published under the title *Man on His Nature* (1940).

Thus it came about that Sherrington (by then knighted) turned from cats and chimpanzees to man. The biologist became philosopher and addressed himelf to the mind/body relationship. And increasingly he moved toward a dualist position, adopting in effect the *interactionism* of Descartes.

After his retirement, his scientific work was carried on for some fourteen years by a number of younger men, among them John C. Eccles and Wilder Penfield.

Penfield later paid a superb tribute to Sherrington as a man and as a scientist in an address to the Canadian Neurological Society in Saskatoon in June, 1957. He spoke of Sherrington as a "legend" in the minds of most of those who knew him and his work, and he referred to him as his own personal "scientific hero."[41]

He states that Sherrington had a knack of always presenting both sides of each physiological problem in the classroom, often leaving his hearers in a state of frustrated confusion! As a student, he sometimes wished that Sherrington would "hide his doubts beneath a shining mantle of authority" and give his pupils a greater sense of security. But it was not Sherrington's way. He had a broad mind and a brilliant one and a memory that "excelled that of any man I have ever known for accuracy of detail."

In physiology Sherrington had always been a realist, seeking truth openly and as far as possible without bias. Stanley Cobb, one of his distinguished American students, hailed him as the outstanding proponent of dualism after Socrates and Descartes. Ultimately he adopted a belief in the existence of two separate elements—the body and the spirit—in the human constitution. But he was never ready to commit himself as explicitly as two of his outstanding students have since done. He did not have the experimental data that they were to become heir to in making their decision.

While engaged in *active* research, Sherrington had resisted the temptation to adopt a dualist position in the mind/brain controversy. His philosophy was very similar to that of Joseph Needham who, in 1936, had written:

> Biologists find that their work is possible *only* if they define life as a dynamic equilibrium in a polyphasic system consisting of proteins, fats, carbohydrates, lipoids, cycloses, and water.[42]

In short, life is "nothing but" physics and chemistry. Needham underscored this approach to scientific research by saying:

> Mechanism is the backbone of scientific thought in biology, since in science we have to act as if the mechanistic theory of life were true, but we are in no way committed to it as a metaphysically valid statement. . . .
>
> Scientific progress can be made only by those who experiment as if mechanism is true.[43]

From its beginning, this outlook was reinforced not merely by its appeal in terms of conceptual simplicity and manageableness, but by reason of its tremendous success in the extension of technology and of man's control over the natural (i.e., the physical) order. Scientists, rightly enough for their purposes, *ignored* a whole area of reality in their search for power over the forces of nature. They succeeded so well that the public went one step further and began to *deny* what the scientists had merely ignored. Then the scientists, themselves being part of "the public," in due time fell into the same trap and reinforced what the public denied. Mechanism gained a dominating hold, and the spirit of "nothing-but-ism" captured the thinking of many research workers and intellectuals.

This was the environment in which Sherrington began his long career. In the laboratory one finds oneself locked in to this "nothing-but-ism" and "as-if-ism" because the climate of scientific opinion predisposes thinking in this way and because our instruments and techniques have been designed to give us only these kinds of answers. No one wants to be excommunicated from the scientific network by questioning current presuppositions, and financial support cannot be obtained easily for research done in any other kind of spirit.

Thus having concentrated all "design initiatives" upon the *subject* to be investigated, the *tools* with which to investigate, and the *methods* of investigation, we boxed ourselves into a mechanistic approach which forced us to assume that life is merely an extension of matter at a certain level of organization and mindedness is merely an extension of life at a certain level of complexity.

Sherrington Changes His Mind

But progress in understanding has continued. Science has within itself a certain self-correctiveness, though it is slow in action. Those who most wholeheartedly follow Thomas Huxley's advice and "sit down before fact as a little child, [and] follow humbly wherever and whatever abysses nature leads to" do indeed learn and sometimes modify their views very substantially.

Unfortunately, it requires mature reflection and considerable courage for any scientist who cares for his reputation to publicly depart from current orthodoxy. The result is that such shifts are apt to occur only toward the end of a scientist's career and the impact of it is likely to have little effect on his own generation. Max Planck observed: "A new scientific truth does not triumph by convincing its opponents and making them see the light, but rather because its opponents eventually die, and a new generation grows up that is familiar with it."[44] Hence change tends to be rather slow.

Sherrington was a man of genius who was also an essentially humble man in the Huxleyan sense. He rightly excluded any appeal to nonphysical forces when he sought to explain the operations of the nervous system, especially in man. It is clear, however, that in the course of half a century of research he observed a pervasive nonphysical reality that expressed itself in an apparent purposefulness. This suggested a form of mindedness that could not be altogether denied.

To admit such nonphysical and therefore nonquantifiable "forces" in the laboratory is often fatal to research because it invites laziness. What cannot be easily explained in terms of physics and chemistry is not further pursued because it is too easily explained in terms of nonphysical causes which have nothing to do with science. The search for physical causes of such phenomena may be abandoned and the demonstration of strict causality fails, even in areas of research where persistence would have advanced our understanding of nature substantially. So the temptation to admit non-physical reality is regarded as thoroughly unhealthy to scientific progress, as indeed it can be.

In the study of man this sometimes causes very disturbing tensions for the individual who wants to take a *whole* view of reality. In discussion with colleagues it can lead to entirely unsatisfactory and often highly disruptive debate. On the floor of the conference room it can result in recrimination and discreditation, and this *can* be very hurtful to the reputation and career of the young scientist.

As a consequence it is almost always the older scientist who has already established his reputation among his peers and who is in little danger of losing it who can afford to say what he really feels in such sensitive matters. Even though he was already a figure of great stature, Sherrington in his *Man on His Nature* was still very cautious in admitting publicly the doubts that had evidently begun to form in his mind as to whether man could be accounted for in monistic terms. He sometimes seems almost apologetic for his dualistic approach.

But dualism can take more than one form. It could be, Sherrington declared, that what was later by Eccles to be called "the self-conscious mind" or "soul," and by Penfield "the spirit," was a kind of emergent phenomenon arising out of the brain, which at a certain point achieved a kind of independence. Thus, in this volume of reflections, Sherrington admitted somewhat tentatively, "That our being should consist of two fundamental elements offers I suppose no greater inherent improbability than that it should rest on one only."[45]

Scientific Rigor Maintained

In 1968, Penfield, to whom this admission was made by his teacher, commented that he too thought this was the best way to leave the issue. But he himself in due course was far more willing to admit the independence of mind at least operationally, even if not in its independent *origin*. Although it meant stepping across the boundary of strict monism into a belief in the nonphysical reality of mind, he felt that such a "confession" was no reason to assume that critical judgment was being abandoned.

The problem of the origin of mind is a perplexing one for the monist, since mind has to be identified in some *proto* form at some prior stage in the development of life. As we have seen, this is very difficult to do. Regarding the origin of mind, Sherrington wrote in 1940:

> Who shall discover it in the little mulberry-mass [the morula stage] which for each of us is our all a little later than the one-celled stage. . . . Yet who shall deny it in the child which in a few months' time that embryo will become? So conversely, at death it seems to re-emerge into no mind. But it seems to come from nothing and return to nothing. The devolution into nothing seems as difficult as the evolution out of nothing.[46]

We really have two problems here. Did "mind" arise out of mindless matter by a process of emergence, or did it arise out of nothing, by a kind of creation? And of course, what happens to mindedness at death?

As we have seen earlier, long before Sherrington, Claude Bernard (1813-1873) had established a *credo* for physiologists which cast the spirit of research in an iron mold from which it was not to escape for over a century. He had written:

> In living bodies *as in inorganic bodies,* laws are immutable and the phenomena governed by these laws are bound to the conditions on which they exist by a necessity and *absolute determinism*. . . .
>
> A determinism in the conditions of vital phenomena should be one of the axioms of experimenting physicians. If they are thoroughly imbued with the truth of this principle, they will *exclude* all supernatural intervention from their explanations; they will have unshaken faith in the idea that fixed laws govern biological science. . . .
>
> *Determinism* thus becomes the foundation of all scientific progress and criticism.[47] (my emphasis throughout)

Sherrington grew up in this intellectual environment and was, at least in his younger days, perhaps largely unaware of the fog it created. He accepted it and indeed thrived upon it. Yet its limitations must later have become apparent to him. But from long habit of mind he was not able (or willing) to entertain the idea that there might be another world of reality not subject to the instruments of measurement which were designed to investigate only the material world. Perhaps Sherrington could not even admit the existence of a non-material world, but he seems in the end to have come very close to the idea that mind had some transcendent value. Even if it came out of "no-mind," it did not *return* to no-mind when the brain was dissolved. This appears to be the implication of a statement he made to Sir John Eccles five days before he died. "For me now," Sherrington said, "the only reality is the human soul."[48]

Who knows how much was intended beyond the manifest fact that his own body was almost ready for dissolution and he knew it. What vigor remained to him was in his mind.

Whatever was meant, two of his pupils were to carry his own research forward in a freer spirit. Their conclusions have given enormous weight to the dualistic argument with Cartesian interactionist overtones. The mind does not wholly govern the operation of the brain, nor the brain wholly govern what goes on in the mind.

Sherrington's great contribution is that he laid the foundations for the understanding of the operation of the brain and yet did it in such a way that his students were still left free to pursue the even more important study, the nature of the interaction in the mind/brain partnership.

Laying the Experimental Foundations

Chapter Abstract

From Sherrington to Penfield and his observations of "relived" memories which were caused by electrode stimulation of the temporal lobes of fully conscious patients.

chapter five

Laying the Experimental Foundations

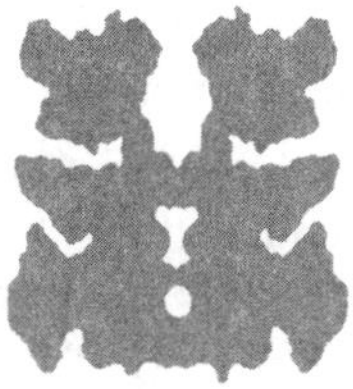

One of Sherrington's most notable pupils was the Canadian neurosurgeon Dr. Wilder Penfield. He is best known for his remarkable studies of, and successful treatment of, hundreds of patients afflicted with epilepsy. This work involved surgical exposure and electrode stimulation of brain tissue in fully conscious patients. By observing the patient's reaction as the electrode was moved gently from point to point over the temporal lobe, it proved possible in many cases to locate the area of damaged tissue causing the epilepsy.

Excising these damaged tissues reduced and sometimes halted the recurrence of fits. An unexpected discovery was the finding that in many cases there was involuntary recall of extremely vivid and often dramatic scenes from the patient's past life, which scenes he or she was able to describe in great detail, being fully conscious of the surgeon's activity. This work was carried out in the Montreal Neurological Institute over a period of thirty years.

In his training at Oxford under Sir Charles Sherrington and for a short period under Dr. Santiago Ramon-y-Cajal in Spain, Penfield absorbed and wholly accepted the principle that all such experimental work must be conducted with the assumption that mind is *in* the brain, that mind will in due course be entirely explained in terms of physics and chemistry and electrical circuitry.

At the close of active surgical practice he observed:

> Throughout my own scientific career, I, like the other scientists, have struggled to prove that the brain accounts for the mind. But now, perhaps, the time has come when we may profitably consider the evidence as it stands, and ask the question: *Do brain-mechanisms account for the mind?* Can the mind be explained by what is now known about the brain? If not, which is the more reasonable of the two possible hypotheses: that man's being is based on one element, or on two?[49]

This shift in point of view was not made easily. In 1950 Penfield outlined briefly but eloquently an entirely mechanistic interpretation of the brain's functioning. But subsequent evidence gradually convinced him that this mechanistic and monistic view did not adequately account for the facts. He wrote subsequently, "Something else finds its dwelling place between the sensory complex and the motor mechanism. . . . There is a switchboard operator as well as a switchboard."[50]

In his *Mystery of the Mind,* there is a frank discussion of the thoughts which went continually through his mind as he probed the brain tissues of epileptic patients in the search for root causes. He wrote that, while agreeing with Lord Adrian that we must always guard against introducing ideas into our science which are not part of science, yet we must subject our research to our own speculation at times and that, when we do, critical evaluation is still possible.[51]

He then describes very briefly the procedure which he came to adopt in the operating room and the rationale behind it. The object was to locate, in epileptic subjects, the cause and location of the point of irritation of the neuron bombardment which is the trigger of the epileptic fit, and, having precisely located it, to excise the tissue in that area. The procedure was found to be successful in hundreds of cases without further ill effect, provided that only one hemisphere had been damaged. The contralateral tissue in the other hemisphere (when the triggering site lay in the temporal lobe) was able to take over the function of the excised tissue. (See Figure 2 for area identity.)

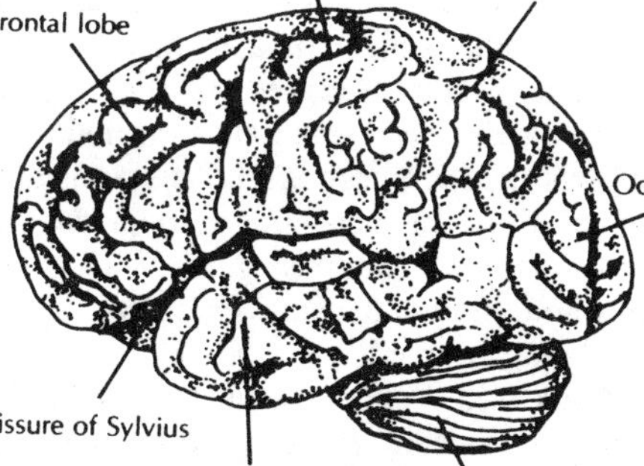

Figure 2. Showing the relation of the temporal lobe to the rest of the brain.

Penfield said further that, for safety's sake and a fair likelihood of cure, the surface of one hemisphere of the brain needs to be bared extensively in order to study and possibly excise a damaged part. This operation was considered less dangerous and more helpful if the patient was conscious and alert during the entire procedure, so only a local painkiller was injected into the patient's scalp. Penfield emphasized that a great amount of doctor-patient trust and communication were necessary to make such an operation both successful and humane.[52] This procedure sometimes revealed the site that caused epileptic seizures by triggering one.

To the layman, it seems an awesome undertaking. But the secret of success depends on the patient's being able to tell the surgeon what his conscious experience is as the operator explores the exposed cerebral tissue with the electrode.* Without this, the only guide to the surgeon would be spasmodic and involuntary muscular

*A single contact point is used, carrying a 60-cycle 2-volt current.

movements. Since the stimulation of the temporal lobe does not produce such movements, only the conscious patient can tell the surgeon of the effects of exploration. (See Figure 3 for map of motor-control areas.)

Double Consciousness

This has produced the surprising and remarkable experience in the subject of a form of *double consciousness,* as Penfield termed it. The patient is not only fully aware of his immediate surroundings, of the operating room, the surgeon and his assistants—the whole local scene in fact—but *also* of the suddenly reenacted scene from the past, a scene so vivid that it includes sounds and in one case even included the odor of coffee being brewed!

He records one such occasion in which "a young South African patient lying on the operating table exclaimed, when he realized what was happening, that it was astonishing to him to realize that he was laughing

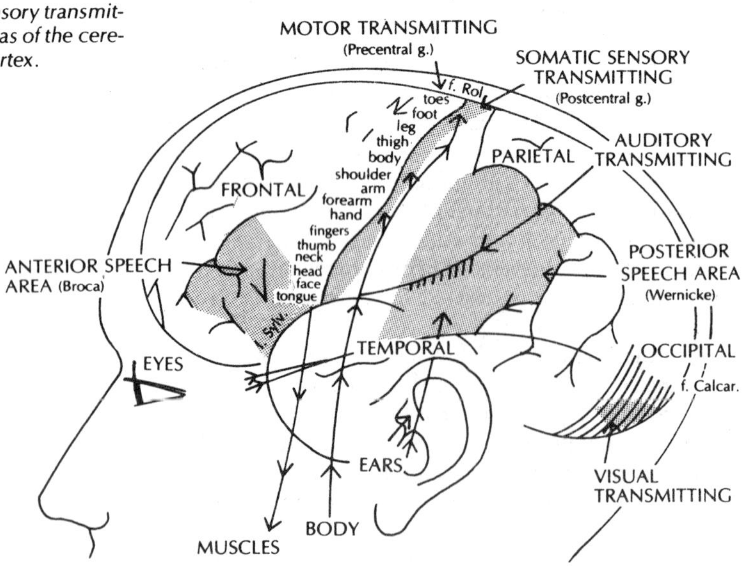

Figure 3. The motor and sensory transmitting areas of the cerebral cortex.

with his cousins on a farm in South Africa, while he was also fully conscious of being in the operating room in Montreal." Penfield observed: "The mind of the patient was as independent of the reflex action as was the mind of the surgeon who listened and strove to understand. Thus, my argument favours independence of mind-action."[53]

Penfield was thus driven to conclude that the stimulus of the electrode was responsible in effect for a kind of TV program which the subject was watching *objectively,* while the subject's own mind was directing the production of an equally complete record of the events occurring in the room around him. Just as we can objectively watch a TV program in the company of others whose presence we are fully conscious of, so here were two different kinds of consciousness. The mind was observing by its own will a program presented to it mechanistically by electrode stimulation much as the TV operated independently of the viewer. As Penfield put it, if we liken the brain to a computer, man *has* a computer, not *is* a computer.[54]

This discovery was totally unexpected. But it was in no way singular. It was repeated again and again for hundreds of patients, each of whom could identify the scene recalled with ease and virtually instantaneously. Patients could elaborate on what they saw and explain the circumstances, much as a TV viewer seeing a serial program might explain the circumstances to a watching companion who was ignorant of the previous events. In such a situation there are clearly two elements. The viewer is *not* part of the TV program but an observer. Yet he is more than an observer insofar as the viewer can adjust the set, clarify the image, change the program, and (in a recall situation) shut it off at will under normal circumstances by a shifting of attention (i.e., turning to another program). Here, then, we have a dualism of object and subject, of brain and mind.

It is no longer safe to view the *mind* as a computer, though the brain is indeed a computer of extraordinary refinement. But this computer has a programmer and an operator who is using it as a tool of recall and of motor control.[55]

Epileptic subjects may sometimes experience times of total "blackout" as to consciousness, the mind apparently ceasing entirely to control the brain. Provided that the brain has already been programmed, the subject becomes an automaton and completes the task in a state of total mindlessness. Patients may even complete a journey from work by car. Provided that the journey is a habitual one and that no unexpected interference occurs, navigating the traffic and road turns is done by means of purely conditioned reflexes; afterwards nothing whatever of the journey will be recalled. The efficiency of the brain as a computer is therefore truly remarkable. Penfield observed that the continual functions of the normally active mind were apparent in such journeys.[56] But he emphasized that it is the mind that must first program the computer brain, since the computer is only a thing and, on its own, has no ability to make totally new decisions for which it is not programmed.[57]

Supervisory Control by the Mind

Wonderful though the brain is as a computer, we see its limitations and its dependence upon the conscious directives of the mind for purposeful levels of activity normal to human life. It is indeed something the individual possesses but not something that possesses the individual.

Penfield was led to believe that only what the mind has "attended to" is apparently programmed into the brain.[58] If the subject has walked through traffic, consciously observing avoidance patterns for maintaining his own safety, this motor activity will be programmed in the computer automatically and in the event of epileptic automatism the subject, though wholly unconscious, will still navigate safely through traffic unless some previously un-experienced complication arises. Penfield described the normally healthy person as an individual who goes about his world constantly depending on his own personal computer, which he programs to fit into his own continually changing objectives and concerns.[59]*

*It should, however, be noted that under hypnosis some recall of details that are only with difficulty attributed to attentive observation in the past is possible. For example, under hypnosis a man described accurately every lump and grain on the top surface of a brick he had

Penfield made many surprising discoveries about the potential of temporal lobe exploration in this way. A particular site when contacted by the electrode produces a specific recollection. It is so specific that the relived experience begins always at precisely the same point in the sequence of events. There is not a continuation where the last scene finished off, but a repeat performance. In one subject this occurred sixty-two successive times![60] This seems to indicate a very specific localization within the cortex, like setting the needle down in the same spot on a record. (See Figures 4 and 5, pages 68 and 69.)

However, it was not always so. One subject, stimulated in the same area, had four apparently unrelated experiential responses. First he heard "footsteps"; secondly, "a company of people in the room"; thirdly, "like being in a gymnasium"; and finally, "a lady talking to a child at the seashore."[61] In the case of repetitious recall, nothing has been lost, nor has anything been added. As Penfield says, "Events are not a bit fancifully elaborated as dreams are apt to be when recalled."[62] And again, elsewhere, Penfield wrote:

> The vividness or wealth of detail and the sense of immediacy that goes with its evoked responses serves to set them apart from the ordinary process of recollection which rarely displays such qualities. Thus with stimulation at Point No. 11 in subject J. V. (Case No. 15) the patient said, "There they go—yelling at me. Stop them!"[63]

The individual is able consciously to identify the meaning of the relived experience not as a kind of hallucination but as something as real as life from which he nevertheless stands apart. A woman listening

---

laid in a wall twenty years before. Since his trade was bricklaying, it is difficult to believe he consciously attended to the surfaces of each brick he laid day by day. Ralph Gerard, who reported this instance, in which the accuracy of reporting was verified because the building was being demolished, observed, "Men remember and recall innumerable details never consciously perceived" ("What is Memory?" *Scientific American*, September 1953, p. 118). It seems unlikely that we *consciously perceive* all that idly strikes our senses. But there is no way of knowing this. Possibly the past is not recoverable in its entirety if only because we would need a second lifetime to recover it, and much of it is worthless.

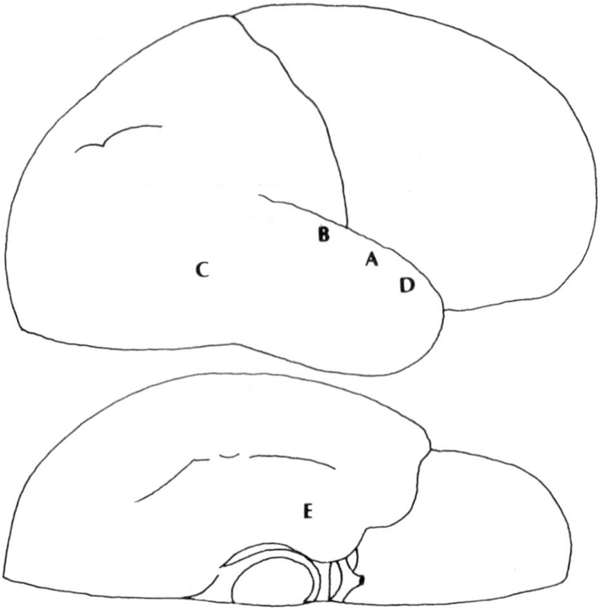

Figure 4. Diagram of the brain of one of Penfield's epileptic patients. (Top: right hemisphere, side view; bottom: right hemisphere, bottom view.) The letters A–E identify points on the brain stimulated by means of an electrode. The verbal responses of the patient to such stimulation are given below. (Reproduced from Penfield, The Mystery of the Mind, *p. 25, with permission.)*

Reaction of patient upon contact at individual points as shown in Figure 4.

A—*"I heard something, I do not know what it was."*

A—*(repeated without warning) "Yes, Sir, I think I heard a mother calling her little boy somewhere. It seemed to be something that happened years ago." When asked to explain, she said, "It was somebody in the neighborhood where I live." Then she added that she herself "was somewhere close enough to hear."*

B—*"Yes. I heard voices down along the river somewhere—a man's voice and a woman's voice calling . . . I think I saw the river."*

C—*"Just a tiny flash of a feeling of familiarity and a feeling that I knew everything that was going to happen in the near future."*

D—*(a needle insulated except at the tip was inserted to the superior surface of the temporal lobe, deep in the fissure of Sylvius, and the current was switched on) "Oh! I had the same very, very familiar memory, in an office somewhere. I could see the desks. I was there and someone was calling to me, a man leaning on a desk with a pencil in his hand."*

I warned her I was going to stimulate, but I did not do so. "Nothing."

E—*(stimulation without warning) "I had a little memory—a scene in a play—they were talking and I could see it—I was just seeing it in my memory."*

to an orchestra under Penfield's stimulating electrode hummed the tune she heard, verse and chorus, thus accompanying by an act of conscious effort the very music which was being recalled so vividly. Such recallings were entirely involuntary. They are not memories voluntarily brought to the surface. They are more detailed and more vivid than such memories ever are. Penfield reports the experience of one patient who reexperienced an occasion on which she was sitting in a room and listening to the children playing outside. The sounds of motor traffic and all the other noises of urban living provided the "natural" background. She discussed all this with Dr. Penfield while it was happening, and so real was the experience that it took some time to convince her afterwards that hé had not actually arranged the whole thing, including the noises outside at the time. Needless to say, he had not done so.[64]

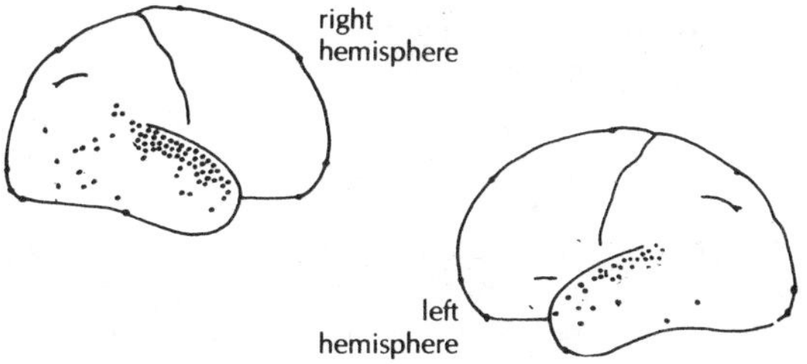

Figure 5. Summary maps to indicate where, in the two cerebral hemispheres, experiential responses of all types were produced by electrical stimulation.

Sometimes the relived experience is so complex that the patient has to explain the background of it later. One 23-year-old woman relived what she called a "fabulous" event when she smashed a plate at dinner time with her elbow and tremendously enjoyed the experience![65] She wanted to explain why she so enjoyed it. Another patient suddenly found herself sitting on the righthand rear seat of a car, with the window slightly down, waiting at a level crossing for a train to pass. She could even count the train cars as they went by, and all the characteristic sounds and noises were there. After the train had passed and they crossed the tracks into town, even an old familiar smell was experienced—the odor of brewing coffee. Penfield says this was the only case of a reexperienced smell that he came across in over a thousand patients whose brain surface was exposed in this way in an effort to locate the cause of epileptic attacks.[66]

Penfield found that if the cortical area which had been the site of stimulation for the reliving of some experience was subsequently removed surgically (when it was believed to be for the benefit of the epileptic patient), the patient could still *voluntarily* recall the experience afterwards. Evidently the memory itself was not at this point but was stored in some area to which the site was connected. Cutting the connection made it impossible to obtain recall by electrical stimulation, but it did not eradicate the memory itself which could still be recalled voluntarily.

Penfield was forced to conclude that, while he had spent years trying to explain the mind totally on the basis of brain-action, his years of study made it far simpler and more logical to explain mind and brain as two basic elements instead of one. This proposition seemed to offer the best path to lead scientists to a final understanding of the brain/mind issue. He believed it would never be possible to explain the mind from neuronal action within the brain, since the mind seems to develop independently throughout a person's life as if it were a continuing thing and since a computer, which the brain is, must have a controlling agency capable of independent comprehension.[67]

Penfield has never suggested that mind can get along without the brain, though clearly brain can continue for some time without mind, as it does in epileptic automatism. But the mind is the agent that programs the brain, that decides what *engrams** shall be encoded in the computer for future retrieval.

Brain Does Not Account for Mind

As Penfield pointed out, and as the monist would expect, if man's being consists of only one fundamental element, then brain neuronal action must account for everything that the mind does.[68] But in that case is there not some evidence of specific neuronal activity corresponding to the *thinking* that the individual is doing? To this Penfield answers no. Such evidence had

*An engram is a memory trace.

not been found in any of his patients. Yet he is careful to admit that there may be such neuronal activity not yet demonstrated. Moreover, he has observed that substantial areas of the cerebral cortex can be removed without any loss of consciousness by the subject even during the operation, a fact which suggests that consciousness is not specifically localized.

He summed up his conclusions by emphasizing that his own surgical experience never revealed any area of gray matter in which local epileptic discharge resulted in what might be described as mind-action.[69]*

Since there is no evidence for such action, Penfield concluded that the only explanation must be that there is indeed another basic element and another form of energy, that as a programmer acts independently of his computer, even if he depends on the computer's action for certain things, so the mind seemingly can act independently of the brain.[70]

If the dualistic view is never explored, we shall never design experimental tools to uncover the mechanism of interaction between the two elements. It therefore seems logical to allow dualism as a working hypothesis and to see whether new avenues of approach to the problem may not be invented in the more open climate that such an allowance would generate. Penfield was convinced we must broaden our hypothetical base.

In this spirit he then turns to a consideration of some more subtle and perhaps more fundamentally important questions that the evidence invites us to ask. He

*The question of whether there is an actual memory trace in the form of RNA specifically relating to each memory is still an open one. The experimental evidence that planaria which have learned some avoidance action have a particular RNA which, when fed to other untaught planaria, gives them a head start in the learning process is still a matter of debate. See for further reading: Arlene L. Harty, Patricia Keith-Lee, and W. D. Morton, "Planaria: Memory Transfer Through Cannibalism Reexamined," *Science* 146 (1964): 274-75; Allan L. Jacobson et al., "Planarians and Memory," *Nature* 209 (1966): 599-601; G. Ungar and L. N. Irwin, "Transfer of Acquired Information by Brain Extracts," *Nature* 214 (1967): 435-55; Ejnar J. Fjerdingstad, *Chemical Transfer of Learned Information* (New York: Elsevier, 1971); R. M. Yaremko and W. A. Hillix, "Reexamination of the Biochemical Transfer of Relational Learning," *Science* 179 (1973): 305.

points out that the history of the mind's development during life as opposed to the brain's course of development is rather different.[71] For example, if one plots a curve showing the excellence of human performance, one sees that the body's performance (and the *brain's*) improves with time as maturing takes place, until after a certain stage in life when a decline begins to set in and ultimately senility. By contrast, the *mind* reveals no characteristic or inevitable decline. In fact, in old age it reaches toward its fullest potential of understanding and judgment, while the body and the brain are slowing and sometimes failing to perform.[72]

He makes a final observation that he had worked as a scientist trying to prove that the mind was accounted for by the brain and, demonstrating as many brain mechanisms as possible, he hoped to show *how* it was thus explained. He ends his reflections by saying:

> In the end I conclude that there is no good evidence, in spite of new methods, such as the employment of stimulating electrodes, the study of conscious patients, and the analysis of epileptic attacks, that the brain alone can carry out the work that the mind does. I conclude that it is easier to rationalize man's being on the basis of two elements than on the basis of one.[73]

Such, then, is the much examined and carefully stated opinion of a man who has had perhaps more firsthand experimental knowledge of the data than any other person at the present time.

The Return of the Whole Person

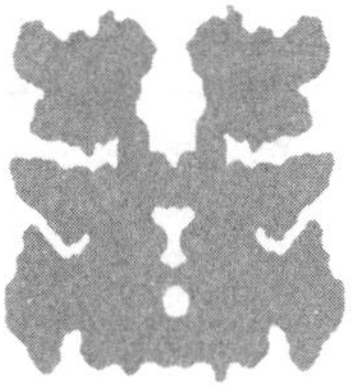

Chapter Abstract

A review of the published dialogue between Popper and Eccles, philosopher and neurophysiologist respectively. By different routes, both men arrive at a basic belief in interactionism, although they disagree on the origin and the destiny of mind or soul.

chapter six

The Return of the Whole Person

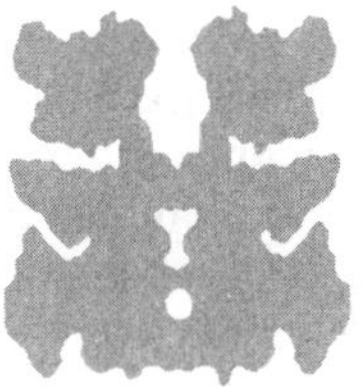

Sherrington's search for the mode of action of mind upon brain was continued not only in Canada by Penfield but also by another of his pupils who became a worthy successor, this time in the British Isles, Sir John C. Eccles.

Eccles, now retired, is considered by many of his peers to be among the world's leading neurophysiologists, and recognition of his stature came in due time when he was made Nobel laureate. For the last twelve years of his long active career in research, Eccles was working in the United States as Director of the Laboratory of Neurobiology at the University of Buffalo Medical School.

His research led him ultimately to adopt a form of interactionism very much like that proposed by Descartes. However, he reached this position on the basis of experimental evidence rather than armchair philosophy. When he retired, he took the opportunity to reflect more deeply on the fruits of his research. Together, Popper and Eccles have now set forth the essence of these reflections in a notable volume entitled *The Self and Its Brain* (referred to earlier).

Evolution of Mind or Creation? Two Routes to the Same End

The format of this volume is unusual. Its unique character stems from the fact that while both men agree as to their main proposition indicated in the subtitle "An Argument for Interactionism," the route by which each came to this position was quite different. They disagree with respect to the origin of the self-conscious mind, and they disagree as to the destiny of it. In the matter of the origin of mind, Popper sees it as almost certainly having an evolutionary origin; Eccles seems to favor some form of creation. In the matter of destiny, Popper holds that we should not commit ourselves beyond the experimental evidence, but should keep an entirely open mind on the question. Eccles is clearly much more committed to the view that the mind or "soul" (as he now calls it) has a destiny beyond the grave for which this present life is strictly preparation.

Popper's view, in essence, is that soul is an evolutionary emergent *somehow* arising out of the activity of the brain, but once formed, having a measure of independence which no longer allows it to be fully described in terms of physics and chemistry. He elaborates this view in the first part of the volume, arguing, for the most part, on philosophical grounds.

In the second part, Eccles presents the essence of his experimental findings and some of his conclusions from a more strictly analytical point of view. Here we find evidence of an essentially scientific nature interpreted in support of the interactionist position, a position adopted by both authors.

Experimental Evidence of the Priority of Will Over Action, of Mind Over Brain

Eccles refers particularly to the work of H. H. Kornhuber as reported in 1974.[74] Kornhuber discovered the existence of electrical potentials generated in the cerebral cortex following the exercise of will to action and *prior* to the actual performance of motor activity. Between the conscious act of will and the activity resulting from it, he consistently observed a measurable interval lasting for a few seconds or less.[75]

In this brief but highly significant interval there is a flurry of electrical potentials over a wide area that gradually centers or concentrates the signals which then bring about the movement willed. This takes the form of "a developing specificity of the patterned impulse discharges" until the pyramidal cells in the relevant cortex area are activated to bring about the desired movement. The delay between willing and willed movement is quite measurable. The nature of the will and the resulting willed action correspond.

The problem remains, however, as to how the neuronal impulses are set in orderly action by the will. One has to assume, Eccles believes, that there is a bridge of some sort "across the interface between the mental world and the physical world."[76] Eccles admits that it is not yet possible to give a scientific account of the nature of this bridge, but holds that Kornhuber's experiments are presumptive experimental evidence that action can indeed be initiated by the will without the introduction of external stimuli in the chain of events leading from one to the other. Moreover, he feels it important to bear in mind that we have the ability to manipulate mental images *without* there being any consequent overt movement. It is thus possible to exercise "will" in two different ways: as imagined movement or as actual response by intent.

Eccles describes Kornhuber's experiments as follows: Elementally simple movements of the index finger were executed by the subject entirely of his own volition, while the very small potentials from the surface of the scalp in the associated control area were accurately timed in respect both to the moment of willing and the moment of responsive movement. The onset of the action potentials resulting from movement of muscles involved in rapid flexing of the finger were used as time markers and compared chronologically with scalp surface potentials. The scalp potentials always preceded the action potentials.

In each case, the subject initiated "*these movements at will* at irregular intervals of many seconds, extreme care being taken to exclude all triggering stimuli"[77] (emphasis mine). It was possible to average from these experiments 250 records of the potentials evoked at each of the several sites over the surface of the scalp. It was found that a "readiness potential" began as a rule about 0.8 seconds before the onset of the muscle action potential specific to the response. It is rather like the effect of the nonspecific warning command given by a sergeant saying, "Company, . . ." before giving the specific command which is to follow. It seems to warn that the will is about to act upon the mechanism. No such warning signal or "attention-getter" seems to be involved when action is *involuntary*. Consciously willed action takes time to be set in motion.

Eccles summarizes Kornhuber's results as follows:

> The trained subjects literally do make the movements in the absence of determining influences from the environment, and any random potentials generated in the relaxed brain would be virtually eliminated by the averaging of 250 traces. Thus we can regard these experiments as providing a convincing demonstration that voluntary movements can be freely initiated independently of any determining influences that are entirely within the neuronal machinery of the brain. If we can regard this as established for elementally simple movements, there is no problem in extending indefinitely the range of consciously wilied or strictly voluntary actions.[78]

Eccles observes that "many other movements of limbs have been investigated with similar results, and even vocalization."[79]

The evidence seems to indicate that "will" initiates a preparatory signal in the brain which is then responsible for the desired movement. Demonstration of interaction can therefore be replicated and always in the same sequential relationships.

The Basic Problem: The Nature of the Interface

Eccles is quick to point out, however, that the outstanding problem which remains lies in the nature of the voluntary control mechanism which bridges "across the interface between the self-conscious mind on the one hand and the modules of the cerebral cortex on the other."[80] The connection from there on in, from cortex to motor neurons, seems clear enough. All we can now say is that *experimental evidence of interactionism does indeed exist.*

Much of what follows in Eccles' treatment is an attempt to map out the problem itself by consideration of current knowledge about the second stage of interaction. The basic problem of the first stage, the mind/brain interaction, still remains.

The last third of the volume is a verbatim record of a series of taped discussions between the two men in which their essential agreement on the reasonableness of the interactionist position is made very clear. Toward the end, however, a clear difference of philosophical approach is indicated by the fact (announced in the Introduction written jointly by the authors) that Popper allows no transcendental leanings to color his thinking, whereas Eccles is clearly willing, and indeed committed, to belief in God and a destiny for the soul beyond death.

We thus have in this volume the interesting case of two highly informed and intelligent men reaching substantial agreement about the nature of the mind/brain relationship but agreeably disagreeing as to the origin of the self-conscious mind and its destiny after death. The points of disagreement served the excellent purpose of sharpening the debate, largely because both men had profound respect for the other's personal bias. One wishes we could all debate such important issues with the same kind of courtesy and restraint!

Insofar as Eccles felt free to follow Penfield in "stepping across the boundary" without abandoning the exercise of "critical judgment," his observations at the end tend to open up broader avenues of discussion and to carry the subject matter of this present study beyond the cold hard facts of the laboratory and into the realm of metaphysics.

Eccles became fully persuaded as a result of his experiments that mind was not an emergent out of brain but somehow an independent observer and user of it. He speaks of the mind as manipulating the brain, of being its master not its servant. The mind searches the brain's store of engrammed information and integrates what it extracts from that store. It is an active search, not just a passive engagement. It can select from the information it scans in the brain and blend the information it acquires into a meaningful whole, rejecting some of the information and modifying it according to its own will. This deliberate process, imposed upon the output of the brain, contributes in turn to the brain's circuitry and capabilities. Hence the title of the volume itself, which was originally planned as *The Self and the Brain,* was by mutual agreement between both authors rewritten as *The Self and* Its *Brain*. The brain is seen as being acted upon by the mind in a purposeful way and as being programmed uniquely by its attached mind merely by reason of the fact that the mind itself is the programmer and programs into the brain only what interests it.

Eccles: Mind Is Autonomous and in Control

Eccles sees mind and brain as a clear-cut dichotomy[81] and goes so far as to equate self-conscious mind with an entity called soul.[82] He rejects the parallelist view[83] as an evasion of the problem. The mind is not merely a viewer of a TV screen who has no control of the TV program. The mind is an active observer who can select the program, change the channels, adjust the color, and even take part in the original programming. There is, he believes, substantial evidence of an active influence of the self-conscious mind upon the neuronal machinery. The mind has no interest in the firings of individual nerve cells any more than the viewer is concerned normally with the functioning of resistors, transistors, condensers, or the circuitry of his own TV set. Such firings of individual nerve cells provide the mind with no useful information in themselves, though *another* mind may be deeply concerned in the event of malfunctioning of the mechanism. It is the collective communal operation of the large number of neurons that has to be the basis of the intelligible and useful readout.[84] This readout is normally a readout-upon-demand and is integrated by the mind into a meaningful message. The brain's TV "picture" is only a *picture* because the mind makes it one.

The mind is by constitution a spectator only rarely and for brief periods. As a rule it is highly involved. This is especially true in creative thinking and in times of deliberate recall. Eccles agrees entirely with Popper's remark in this connection:

I remember is equivalent to *I succeed in remembering*. So only at the moment at which its activity leads to a success is the self really a spectator (and nothing else). Otherwise it is constantly, or almost constantly, active.[85]

Eccles reverted later to the parallelist view and observed:

> We can turn now to other aspects of the basis for our strong dualistic hypothesis. I want to mention just briefly that we have to assume that our self-conscious mind has some coherence with the neuronal operations of the brain, but we have furthermore to recognize that it is not in a passive relationship. It is an active relationship searching and also modifying the neuronal operations. So this is a very strong dualism and it separates completely our theory from any parallelistic views where the self-conscious mind is passive. That is the essence of the parallelistic hypothesis.
>
> All varieties of identity theories imply that the mind's conscious experiences have merely a passive relationship as a spin-off from the operations of the neural machinery, which themselves are self-sufficient. These operations give the whole motor performance, and in addition give all conscious experiences and memory retrievals. Thus on the parallelistic hypotheses the operations of the neural machinery provide a necessary and sufficient explanation of all human actions.[86]

Popper: There Is an Active "Ghost in the Machine"

With this overall assessment of the situation Popper agreed—a fact which suggests that Eccles' dualism was not the result of his wishful acceptance of the reality of a spiritual world, since Popper statedly does not admit any such world. Nevertheless, he thus far agrees with Eccles as to say with respect to the above:

> That is exactly what I tried to express when, with a feeling of despair, I said in Oxford in 1950 that I believe in the ghost in the machine. That is to say, I think that the self in a sense plays on the brain, as a pianist plays on a piano or as a driver plays on the controls of a car.[87]

This called forth from Eccles the following summary of his own personal conclusions based on many years of active research:

As a challenge, I will present a very brief summary or outline of the theory as I see it. Here it is. The self-conscious mind is actively engaged in reading out from the multitude of active centres at the highest level of brain activity, namely in the liaison brain. The self-conscious mind selects from these centres according to attention and interest and from moment to moment integrates its selection to give unity even to the most transient conscious experiences. Furthermore, the self-conscious mind acts upon those neural centres, modifying the dynamic spatio-temporal patterns of the neural events. Thus in agreement with Sperry, it is postulated that the self-conscious mind exercises a superior interpretative *and* controlling role upon the neural events.[88] (emphasis mine)

To this Popper replied:

I think that is very good. The only place where perhaps one should seek to make it even stronger is where you speak of the liaison brain; namely, we could make it stronger by making it clear that the liaison brain is, as it were, almost an object of choice of the self-conscious mind. . . .

So I go even a little further than you in my interactionism, in that I look at the very location of the liaison brain as being the result of interaction between the brain and the self-conscious mind.[89]

Mind as an Evolutionary "Outcrop": A Biologically Irrational View

Subsequently in the course of this dialogue, Eccles made what seems to be a very important observation for those who propose that self-consciousness was an advantage to its possessor and was therefore an evolutionary outcrop that was favored by selective pressures. Apart from the fact that many forms of life below man—forms which can hardly be credited with self-consciousness—seem to have a far better chance of survival than man does, the derivative of self-conscious mind seems unlikely for another reason.

There is on the parallelist view no biological reason whatsoever why the self-conscious mind should have evolved at all. If it can do nothing, what is the evolutionary meaning of it? . . . It can only have survival value if it can *do* things.[90] (emphasis mine)

Of course, if mind can act upon brain in this dualistic sense as an independent force, then will can act upon matter without being rooted in the matter it is acting upon. Such a concept raises disturbing possibilities in physics and, in fact, could—as Eccles himself suggests—involve a veritable transformation of physics.[91] Eccles quotes an observation by Erwin Schrödinger in 1967 apropos of such a contingency:

> The impasse *is* an impasse. Are we thus not the doers of our deeds? Yet we feel responsible for them, we are punished or praised for them, as the case may be. It is a horrible antinomy. I maintain that it cannot be solved on the level of present-day science which is still entirely engulfed in the "exclusion principle" (i.e., the exclusion of all forces save physical ones). . . . The scientific attitude would have to be rebuilt, science must be made anew.[92]

At the close of this dialogue there are questions that carry us beyond the range of science and perhaps even beyond the range of philosophy. Thus he says:

> I wanted to stress this pre-eminence of the self-conscious mind because now I raise the questions: What is the self-conscious mind? How does it come to exist? How is it attached to the brain in all its intimate relationships of give and take? How does it come to be? And in the end, not only how does it come to be, but what is its ultimate fate when, in due course, the brain disintegrates?[93]

The Origin of Mindedness Remains a Mystery

So he observes that the poignant problem confronting each person in his life is his attempt to become reconciled with his inevitable end in death. The inevitability of death affects man uniquely because in his development he has become self-conscious. In his book *Facing Reality* Eccles made the following observation, which he now quotes:

> I believe that there is a fundamental mystery in my existence, transcending any biological account of the development of my body (including my brain) with its genetic inheritance and its evolutionary origin. . . . I cannot believe that this wonderful gift of a conscious existence has no further future, no possibility of another existence under some other unimaginable conditions.[94]

Later he says:

> Our coming-to-be is as mysterious as our ceasing-to-be at death. Can we therefore not derive hope because our ignorance about our origin matches our ignorance about our destiny? Cannot life be lived as a challenging and wonderful adventure that has meaning yet to be discovered?[95]

Eccles concludes that science has gone too far in breaking down man's belief in his spiritual potential and giving him the idea that he is merely an insignificant material being in the frigid cosmic immensity,[96] a phrase perhaps inspired (if that is the word) by Jacques Monod's bleak picture of the future in his *Chance and Necessity*.

The following morning Eccles felt it desirable to sharpen the issue by saying:

> If [mind] is an emergent derivative of simply a brain developed to the highest level in the evolutionary process, then I think, we give way finally to a view that makes the self-conscious mind simply a spin-off from the highly developed brain. . . .
>
> My position is this. I believe that my personal uniqueness, that is, my own experienced self-consciousness, is not accounted for by this emergent explanation of the coming-to-be of my own self. It is the *experienced* uniqueness that is not so explained. . . .
>
> So I am constrained to believe that there is what we might call a supernatural origin of my unique self-conscious mind or my unique selfhood or soul; and that gives rise of course to a whole new set of problems.
>
> By this idea of supernatural creation I escape from the incredible improbability that the uniqueness of my own self is genetically determined. There is no problem about the genetic uniqueness of my brain. It is the uniqueness of the experienced self that requires this hypothesis of an independent origin of the self or soul, which is then associated with a brain, *that so becomes MY brain*.[97] (emphasis mine)

Brain, Not the Cause of Mind, but Its Conditioner

The brain is not, therefore, the physiological *cause* of the self, but, as Viktor Frankl put it, it does *condition* it.[98] There is a great difference between causing and conditioning.

The position which both Popper and Eccles take is one of interactionism, the mind governing and employing the brain as a necessary device for its own conscious purposes, but also being in turn influenced by the brain's efficiency, limitations, genetic endowment, and healthy or diseased condition. The brain is limited in its programming by the mind: the mind is limited in its program by the efficiency and capacity of the brain as a machine. There is an interaction but there is a separation between the two parties to the arrangement. The mind, if Eccles is right, is not an emergent, a spin-off, an "arm" of the brain. It exists in its own right.

Penfield found himself driven by the evidence to ask similar fundamental questions and quite independently came tentatively to rather similar conclusions.

He questioned what becomes of the mind following death. Without a brain, the mind is finally robbed of the instrument essential to its operation. What happens then? All that can be said with any certainty is that the brain has not yet fully accounted for the mind, and perhaps mind can carry on afterwards without it.

If mind is dependent on brain for its operation insofar as that operation requires some form of energy, whence would that energy come from in the absence of brain? Penfield suggests that perhaps the disintegration of the brain in death sets the mind free to tap some other form of energy. Unless this is so, it would seem that after death, mind must vanish. Can it establish connection with "another source of energy" outside the measurable world?[99]

Penfield seems to have in mind a new source of energy and a new source of life. This is not to be equated with pantheism, for the mind itself seems to have acquired a self-conscious personal identity that persists even when gross damage is done to the brain.

He cautiously suggests that perhaps even during life some of this new energy comes directly from God Himself.[100]

Origins and Destinies

The mind of man is such that the idea of personal annihilation by death is both hard to conceive and hard to accept. We have seen that mystery surrounds the *origin* of the mind, and mystery assuredly surrounds its *destiny*. Since it seems impossible for us to achieve certainty in the matter of origin by scientific means, there is even less likelihood of achieving certainty in the matter of destiny by scientific means. Where, then, shall we continue the search, since it is inevitable that we shall do so?

Beyond Philosophy

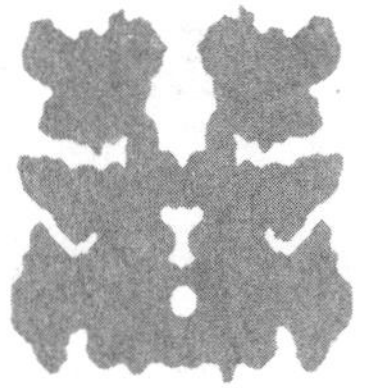

Epilogue Abstract

A consideration of the origin and the destiny of mind, looking beyond scientific enquiry to biblical revelation and theology. A centuries-old biblical view is weighed beside modern views of dualistic interactionism.

epilogue

Beyond Philosophy

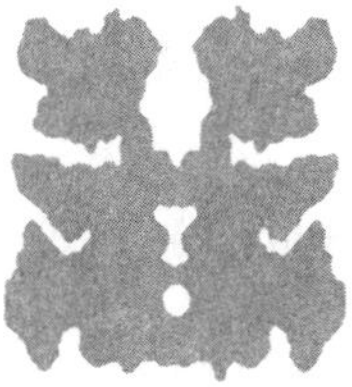

Since the search for origins and the search for destinies are both admittedly outside the province of scientific enquiry, it seems we are left with only metaphysical speculation. But such speculation has not led to any profound certainty hitherto. It is clear that it lacks the kind of raw data with which science proceeds toward understanding. Where, then, is this data to be found?

The usual reply is: Ask those who have experienced the "blowing out of the candle" and returned. But this source of information is unsatisfactory because it varies so widely from person to person and there is no absolute assurance that the candle was really blown out in the first place. We seem to be left with no alternative but to turn to biblical revelation, a remarkable account which has carried untold millions who were guided by it through the most severe testings imaginable with an absolute assurance of survival in peace and joy on the other side of the grave.

Where Revelation Seems Necessary

Now metaphysical speculation is the search for understanding by the use of reason alone without the help of revelation, whereas theology is the application of philosophy to religious experience by the use of reason but *with* the help of revelation. If this added source of data is allowed, we may perhaps usefully take a second look at what biblical theology has been saying for centuries on the mind/brain or soul/body relationship. And let us do so with special attention to its statements on what happens when the mind has been deprived by death of the body upon which it has depended for expression.

Man: A Dichotomy of Mind and Body

First, it can be stated without equivocation that biblical theology has always viewed man as a hyphenate creature, a spirit/body dichotomy. This is the clear position taken in the Old and New Testaments. To this extent there is no quarrel between theology and the findings of recent research. Moreover, the Bible has always viewed death as being quite simply the separation of these two constituents. When the spirit or soul* leaves the body, the body is dead.

Furthermore, both Testaments agree in seeing the union of the two as essential to the real existence of the whole person as such. Hence the tremendous emphasis upon the resurrection of the body throughout the Bible. If revelation was correct in this emphasis upon the union of the two constituents, perhaps it is also correct in what it reveals about the destiny of the individual after death.

It must be borne in mind that it was the Greek philosophers, not the Christian theologians, who viewed the body as a prison of the soul. Since Eccles uses the words *mind* and *soul* interchangeably (as the theologians have used the words *soul* and *spirit* interchangeably), all are addressing themselves to the same issue.

**Soul* and *spirit* are equated in French by the use of a single word, *âme*, a word also meaning *person*. And *mind* and *spirit* are likewise equated in the word *esprit*. So also in German the single word *Seele* can mean either mind or soul.

European theologians have been particularly concerned to underscore that the body is the instrument whereby the soul or mind fulfills itself and achieves self-expression. In exchange, the soul or mind gives to the body the potential for purposeful activity. The epileptic automaton's capabilities exist only because the mind has already programmed the brain purposefully. Though the clinically dead may be kept alive for some time by heroic measures, it is clear that the body is essentially purposeless in its activity in the absence of mindedness.

Mind and Body: Each Suited to the Other

Mind or soul provides the brain with a significant, meaningful, and ordered economy. Brain makes the soul *effective* in return. The soul finds fulfilling expression via the body through interaction with the brain. The soul therefore animates the body. By separating the two, both suffer "death." Insofar as the person as a *whole* is concerned, the Bible clearly indicates a form of severance that is not to be undone until the body is resurrected and united with the soul. The problem is that physical resurrection has tended to be played down, buried as it were beneath the overemphasis upon the survival of the spirit. But in the light of present knowledge we cannot reasonably reconstitute the whole man without resurrecting his body, since bodily existence seems essential to that wholeness. It is therefore not surprising that in the absence of a firm hope of bodily resurrection the experience of death is faced with such abhorrence, since it is the dissolution of a partnership of mind and brain essential to personal survival. My body is my soul's proper home. My soul is my body's proper master. They belong together.

Throughout the Christian era, theologians have held that the soul is a creation. It seems difficult to account for it in any other way as far as present evidence goes.* But there also seems to be a certain "niceness of fit" between soul and body. There is interaction, not just parallel and independent development. Abraham

*Popper's view is that mind (which is equivalent to soul in this context) simply appeared. But this really tells us nothing. It has no explanatory value whatever, and although it may be an escape from creationism such a statement in itself has no more scientific validity than the plain statement that the soul is created. Both are expressions of a faith.

Kuyper (1837-1920), a Dutch theologian, held that "God creates the soul in the embryo which had a predisposition towards the soul predestined for it."[101] The throwing of the dice to determine the genetic endowment is not therefore altogether left to chance.

Since the child receives his genes from his parents, he has a head start toward the kind of personality he can develop. If he is musically equipped he is likely to become musically inclined, provided that circumstances allow the means as he grows up. He does not start therefore as a *tabula rasa* but with a certain framework within which the soul will give itself expression. Kuyper was very specific. The soul is indeed created *ex nihilo* by God, but not in an arbitrary form. It is created in *this* man, at *this* time in world history, in *this* country, in *this* particular family or race, and therefore with the potential characteristics and, to some extent, limitations which such specific matching implies.

The Subject Half and the Object Half

Theologians speak of the dual nature of man as being comprised of an *object* half and a *subject* half. The object half is termed in the New Testament the soma, the subject half the pneuma. Together they constitute "soul" or selfhood, the individual, the person. Karl Barth held that soul and body are distinguished from each other as subject and object, the subject having the unique capability of being able to know both itself and its objective body. Materialism with its denial of the soul makes man subjectless and therefore only a half-entity, while spiritualism with its denial of the body makes him objectless and therefore only a half-entity. Either view effectively annihilates man as man.

Any system of psychology which tries to make either of these half-entities swallow up the other, is no longer dealing with man as such. Behaviorism is not therefore a psychology of man but only of man's object half. Man *has* a computer, not *is* a computer, as Penfield concludes; and to treat him as a computer is like saying that a love letter should be the sole object of one's affection—not the sender.

**Death:
The Rending Apart
of Mind and Body**

Revelation makes it very clear that when the soul or spirit leaves the body, the body is dead (James 2:26) and that if the spirit is somehow *returned* to the body, the whole person comes back to life (Luke 8:55). This duality is repeated in hundreds of places in the Bible (cf. for example, Matthew 26:41; Romans 8:10; 1 Corinthians 5:5; 6:20; 7:34; 2 Corinthians 7:1; Galatians 5:17). Indeed the formation of Adam as the first *human* being is expressly stated as the result of the animation of a body by a spirit, constituting it as a living soul (Genesis 2:7).

As to the state of the soul on the other side of the grave, we seem to find ourselves dependent entirely on revelation. Revelation provides us with the only consistent picture we have. Without it we really know nothing except by extrapolation beyond the experimental evidence. The New Testament assures us of the resurrection of the body and Paul elaborates on the nature of this body (1 Corinthians 15:35-44). And we have the most complete picture of the potential of this resurrection body by observing what is said of Jesus Christ after *His* resurrection, knowing from Paul (Philippians 3:20-21) that this is the kind of body *we* also may have, depending upon our relationship to Him during our life in this world.

Here we see a body that can pass freely through material barriers, locked doors, and so forth, yet can be handled and examined for purposes of identification. It will be a body capable of communication with the physical world—speaking, being seen, heard, and felt; and it will be fully recognizable. It will be a body capable of sharing a meal, eating food, and then vanishing at will only to reappear in some other location.

It will be a body that can act upon the physical world, moving objects, making accurate predictions, going for walks, and (it would seem) even building and lighting a fire in preparation for a meal. Such potential seems to make possible virtually all that our bodies can do and much more besides in terms of movement within and through the material world. One could scarcely dream of greater freedom from the limitations of our present existence without apparently sacrificing any of its advantages. Such a body will surely open up vast new areas of human activity—everywhere in the universe.

Such a Resurrection Is Uniquely the Christian Hope

It is, in fact, the Christian hope. And it is not a kind of pious hope but highly specific. It will in some way be *our* body animated by *our* spirit and therefore truly and identifiably *our*selves.

Such a hope was once shared by people in every walk of life and it made life bearable in otherwise unbearable circumstances. Today it is a hope that struggles to stay alive against an enormous negative pressure brought into existence very largely by the scientific community. Even humanists themselves are beginning to wonder whether we may not have been misled by an unwarranted commitment to a mechanistic view of life and a materialistic philosophy which seems unavoidably to accompany it.

Writing in the *Bulletin of Atomic Scientists,* Professor Roger W. Sperry, a psychologist at the California Institute of Technology, observed:

> Before science, man used to think himself a free agent possessing free will. Science gives us, instead, causal determinism wherein every act is seen to follow inevitably from preceding patterns of brain excitation. Where we used to see purpose and meaning in human behaviour, science now shows us a complex bio-physical machine composed entirely of material elements, all of which obey inexorably the universal laws of physics and chemistry. . . .
>
> I find that my own conceptual working model of the brain leads to inferences that are in direct disagreement with many of the foregoing; especially I must take issue with that whole general materialistic-reductionist conception of human nature and mind that seems to emerge from the currently prevailing objective analytic approach in the brain-behaviour sciences.
>
> When we are led to favour the implications of modern materialism in opposition to older, more idealistic values in these and related matters, I suspect that science may have sold society and itself a somewhat questionable bill of goods.[102]

It may have, indeed.

Response

LEE EDWARD TRAVIS

A dominating assumption held by psychologists today is that the human being is body and nothing more and what is real can be perceived only by the sense organs or by a physical instrument. Based on this assumption, persons are essentially totally defined by the physical parts that constitute them and to know them one must ultimately understand their anatomy and their physiology. They can be reduced completely to physics and chemistry, and there is nothing left over.

The ordinary person does not share this assumption. Such people believe that there is something else, that there is a conscious mind that takes control, possibly even of one's whole life, and to a large degree determines one's destiny. It is true, they think, that genetics plays a large role in one's development and that chance enters into the picture. But mainly they believe that consciousness faithfully attends them as long as they live and reluctantly leaves at their death to live on forever in another world. Scientists and philosophers have too quickly dismissed the testimony of the common person about his or her experience. As a scientist Dr. Custance not only respects the common person but also solicits the aid of other noted scientists to tell of their lifelong work on mind-body problems.

One could say either that the brain produces the mind as an epiphenomenon, the melody that floats from the harp, or that the mind programs the brain, using it as a faithful servant in the complicated job of living. The evidence that Dr. Custance gives us strongly supports the second possibility. It comes largely from the great works of two men, the neurosurgeon Wilder Penfield and the neurophysiologist John C. Eccles.

Penfield would stimulate electrically the proper motor cortex of conscious patients and challenge them to keep one hand from moving when the current was applied. The patient would seize this hand with the other hand and struggle to hold it still. Thus one hand under the control of the electrical current and the other hand under the control of the patient's mind fought against each other. Penfield risked the explanation that the patient had not only a physical brain that was stimulated to action but also a nonphysical reality that interacted with the brain. Could this nonphysical reality be the mind? With other patients being stimulated in other cortical areas, a double consciousness was produced. Patients, while being fully aware of their immediate surroundings on the operating table, were also experiencing a suddenly reenacted scene from the past, a scene so clear that it included sounds and even the odor of coffee being brewed. Penfield considered such double-consciousness experiences as an argument for independent mind action, for a dualism of object and subject and for a separateness of brain and mind.

Eccles became fully persuaded after his lifelong work in neurophysiology that mind was not an emergent out of the brain but somehow an independent programmer of it. The mind acts on the brain in a purposeful, manipulating, and actively creative way. Dr. Custance draws attention to the congruity between the revelation of Scripture and the conclusions of these two modern scientists.

Both the Old and the New Testaments proclaim the union of the mind and the body as essential to the existence of the whole person. The Bible sees a form of severance between the mind and the body at death that will be neither undone *nor* remedied until the body is resurrected and united with the mind. For the whole person as portrayed in the Bible the mind and the body belong together, always with the former as master and the latter as servant. Behaviourism is not a psychology of man but only of man's object self. Man *has* a computer, not *is* a computer.

I like Dr. Custance's beautiful description of the new body to which the mind is returned when the whole person comes back to life. Basically his description is based on the story of Jesus Christ after his resurrection.

I believe this little book is sound and stimulating, and I will plan to use it in my classes.

References

[1]Karl R. Popper and John C. Eccles, *The Self and Its Brain* (New York: Springer-Verlag, 1977), p. viii.

[2]Wilder Penfield, in the "Control of the Mind" Symposium, held at the University of California Medical Center, San Francisco, 1961, quoted in Arthur Koestler, *Ghost in the Machine* (London: Hutchinson Publishing Group, 1967), pp. 203-4.

[3]Chuang Chou, quoted in Edward H. Schafer, *Ancient China,* in the Time-Life series *Great Ages of Man* (New York: Time-Life Books, 1967), p. 62.

[4]Paul Weiss, in discussion of J. R. Smythies's paper "Some Aspects of Consciousness," in *Beyond Reductionism,* ed. Arthur Koestler and J. R. Smythies (London: Hutchinson Publishing Group, 1969), p. 252.

[5]Lord Adrian, guest editorial, "The brain as physics," *Science Journal,* vol. 3, no. 5 (May 1967), p. 3.

[6]Claude Bernard, quoted in Seymour S. Kety, "A Biologist Examines the Mind and Behavior," *Science* 132 (1960): 1863.

[7]Thomas Huxley, "On the Physical Basis of Life," *Lay Sermons* (n.p., 1870), p. 152.

[8]Thomas Huxley, "Mr. Darwin's Critics," *Contemporary Review* (November 1871), p. 464.

[9]Huxley, "Descartes," *Lay Sermons,* p. 371.

[10]Arthur O. Lovejoy, *The Great Chain of Being* (New York: Harper and Row, 1960).

[11]See Chauncey D. Leake, "Perspectives in Adaptation: Historical Background" in *Handbook of Physiology,* sec. 4 (Washington, D. C.: American Physiological Society, 1964), pp. 5-6.

[12]J. R. Smythies, "Some Aspects of Consciousness," in *Beyond Reductionism,* eds. Arthur Koestler and J. R. Smythies (London: Hutchinson Publishing Group, 1969), p. 235.

[13]W. H. Thorpe, *Animal Nature and Human Nature* (London: Methuen, 1974), p. 310.

[14]David Bidney, *Theoretical Anthropology* (New York: Columbia University Press, 1953), p. 3.

[15]Stanley Cobb, quoted in A. I. Hallowell, "Self, Society, and Culture in Phylogenetic Perspective," in *Evolution After Darwin*, ed. Sol Tax, vol. 2 (Chicago: University of Chicago Press, 1960), p. 348.

[16]Cyril Ponnamperuma, "Chemical Evolution and the Origin of Life," *Nature* 201 (1964): 337.

[17]D. F. Lawden, in Letters to the Editor under Biology, *Nature* 202 (1964): 412.

[18]H. S. Jennings, *Behavior of the Lower Organisms*, Columbia University Biological Series 10 (New York: Columbia University Press, 1915), p. 334.

[19]Ibid., p. 335.

[20]Ibid., p. 336.

[21]J. Boyd Best, "Protopsychology," *Scientific American* (February 1963), p. 62.

[22]Lovejoy, *Chain of Being*, p. 276.

[23]J.-B.-R. Robinet, *De La Nature* 4 (Paris, 1776): 11-12.

[24]Sir Julian Huxley, "Genetics, Evolution and Human Destiny," in *Genetics in the Twentieth Century*, ed. L. C. Dunn (New York: Macmillan, 1951), pp. 604-5.

[25]Theodosius Dobzhansky, in "Book Reviews," *Science* 175 (7 January 1972): 49.

[26]E. W. Sinnott, *Cell and Psyche: The Biology of Purpose* (Chapel Hill: University of North Carolina Press, 1950), pp. 48-50.

[27]Dobzhansky, in "Book Reviews," p. 49.

[28]Theodosius Dobzhansky, "Man Consorting with Things Eternal," in *Science Ponders Religion*, ed. H. Shapley (New York: Appleton-Century-Crofts, 1960), pp. 120-21.

[29]C. H. Waddington, Book Review, *Discovery* (October 1960), p. 453.

[30]Sir Charles Sherrington, *Man on His Nature* (Cambridge: Cambridge University Press, 1963), p. 251.

[31]Ibid., p. 65.

[32]Edward McCrady, *Religious Perspectives of College Teaching in Biology* (New Haven, Conn.: Edward W. Hazen Foundation, 1950), pp. 19-20.

[33]Sir Alister Hardy, *The Living Stream* (London: Collins, 1965), p. 257.

[34]Lewis Thomas, *The Lives of a Cell* (New York: Viking, 1974), p. 13.

[35]Ashley Montagu, *On Being Human* (New York: Henry Schuman, 1951), p. 34.

[36]Nicholas Seeds and Albert E. Vetter, *Proceedings of the National Academy of Science* 68, p. 3219; L. W. Lapham and W. R. Markesbury, "Human Fetal Cerebellar Cortex: Organization and Maturation of Cells in Vitro," *Science* 173 (27 August 1971): 829-32.

[37]Isaac Harary, "Heart Cells in Vitro," *Scientific American* (May 1962), pp. 141-52.

[38]Paul Weiss and A. C. Taylor, "Reconstruction of Complex Organs from Single Cell Suspensions of Chick Embryos in Advanced Stages of Differentiation," *Proceedings of the National Academy of Science* 46 (September 1960): 177-85.

[39]Graham Chedd, "Cellular Samaritans," *New Scientist*, (31 October 1968), p. 256.

[40]Popper and Eccles, *The Self*, p. 69.

[41]This is reprinted in Penfield's *Second Career* (Toronto: Little, Brown, 1963), pp. 66-75.

[42]Joseph Needham, quoted in Theodore H. Savory, *Mechanistic Biology and Animal Behaviour* (London: Watts, 1936), title page.

[43]Ibid., p. 170.

[44]Max Planck, *Scientific Autobiography and Other Papers* (New York: Greenwood, 1968), pp. 33-34.

[45]Sir Charles Sherrington, quoted in Wilder Penfield, "Engrams in the Human Brain: Mechanisms of Memory," *Proceedings of the Royal Society of Medicine* (August 1968), reprinted by Montreal Neurological Institute as Reprint No. 934, p. 3.

[46]Sherrington, *Man on His Nature*, p. 210.

[47]Claude Bernard, *An Introduction to the Study of Experimental Medicine*, trans. H. C. Greene (New York: Henry Schuman, 1949), p. 69.

[48]Popper and Eccles, *The Self*, p. 558.

[49]Wilder Penfield, *The Mystery of the Mind* (Princeton: Princeton University Press, 1975), p. xiii.

[50]Wilder Penfield, *The Physical Basis of Mind*, ed. P. Laslett (Oxford: Basil Blackwell, 1950), p. 64.

[51]Penfield, *The Mystery*, pp. 4-5.

[52]Ibid., p. 12.

[53]Ibid., p. 55.

[54]Ibid., p. 108.

[55]Ibid., p. 40.

[56]Ibid., p. 45.

[57]Ibid., p. 47.

[58]Ibid., pp. 39-40, 58-59.

[59]Ibid., p. 61.

[60]Wilder Penfield and Phanor Perot, "The Brain's Record of Auditory and Visual Experience: A Final Summary and Discussion," *Brain,* vol. 86, part 4 (December 1963), p. 685.

[61]Ibid., p. 682.

[62]Wilder Penfield, "Epilepsy; Neurophysiology and Some Brain Mechanisms Related to Consciousness," in *Basic Mechanisms in Epilepsies,* eds. Jasper, Ward, and Pope (Toronto: Little, Brown, 1969), p. 796.

[63]Penfield and Perot, "The Brain's Record," p. 679.

[64]Ibid., pp. 645-46.

[65]Ibid., p. 643.

[66]Ibid., pp. 648-49.

[67]Penfield, *The Mystery,* p. 80.

[68]Ibid., p. 78.

[69]Ibid., pp. 77-78.

[70]Ibid., pp. 79-80.

[71]Ibid., p. 86.

[72]Ibid., p. 87.

[73]Ibid., p. 113.

[74]H. H. Kornhuber, "Cerebral Cortex, Cerebellum, and Basal Ganglia: An Introduction to Their Motor Functions," in *The Neurosciences: Third Study Program,* eds. F. O. Schmitt and F. G. Worden (Cambridge, Mass.: Massachusetts Institute of Technology, 1973), pp. 267-80.

[75]Popper and Eccles, *The Self,* p. 283.

[76]Ibid., p. 285.

[77]Ibid., p. 283.

[78]Ibid., p. 294.

[79]Ibid., p. 283. An avenue of light on the relationship between thought and action that Eccles does not mention might be the finding, known for some years, that unspoken thought is nevertheless accompanied by small detectable movements of the vocal chords. When the congenitally deaf think (those who use sign language), these same potential movements can be demonstrated in the finger muscles rather than in the vocal chords. In reviewing A. N. Sololov's *Inner Speech and Thought* (Moscow, 1968), Katherine S. Harris observes that electromyographic indicators of this sort may simply represent some kind of "overflow phenomenon." This would seem to be further evidence of interactionism—the flow of thought initiating vocal expression involving muscular activity that is not only unwanted but as far as possible suppressed. See J. C. Nunnally and R. L. Flaugher, "Psychological Implications of Word Usage," *Science* 140 (1963): 775. For Harris, see *Science* 176 (1972), "Book Reviews" under "Silent Articulation."

[80]Popper and Eccles, *The Self,* p. 294.

[81]Ibid., p. 471.

[82]Ibid., p. 560.

[83]Ibid., p. 474.

[84]Ibid., p. 477.

[85]Ibid., p. 488.

[86]Ibid., p. 494.

[87]Ibid., pp. 495-96.

[88]Ibid., p. 495.

[89]Ibid.

[90]Ibid., p. 516.

[91]Ibid., p. 543.

[92]Erwin Schrödinger, *What Is Life? and Mind and Matter* (Cambridge: Cambridge University Press, 1967), pp. 131-32.

[93]Popper and Eccles, *The Self,* pp. 552-53.

[94]John C. Eccles, *Facing Reality* (New York: Springer-Verlag, 1970), p. 83.

[95]Ibid., chapter 5.

[96]Popper and Eccles, *The Self,* p. 558.

[97]Ibid., pp. 559-60.

[98]Viktor Frankl, in discussion of J. R. Smythies's paper, "Some Aspects of Consciousness" in *Beyond Reductionism,* ed. Arthur Koestler and J. R. Smythies (London: Hutchinson Publishing Group, 1969), p. 254.

[99]Penfield, *The Mystery,* p. 88.

[100]Ibid., p. 89.

[101]Abraham Kuyper, quoted in G. C. Berkouwer, *Man: The Image of God* (Grand Rapids: Eerdmans, 1963), p. 290.

[102]Roger W. Sperry, "Mind, Brain, and Humanist Values," *Bulletin of the Atomic Scientists* (September 1966), pp. 2-3.

For Further Reading

Books

Eccles, Sir John C. **Facing Reality.** Springer Verlag International, 1970.

This is subtitled "Philosophical Adventures of a Brain Scientist," and it would be difficult to describe the volume more aptly. It is at times a rather technical study that requires some dedication, but it is relieved throughout by what must surely strike the reader as both brilliant and refreshing excursions into some of the more philosophical aspects of mind/brain interaction.

Koestler, Arthur and Smythies, J. R., eds. **Beyond Reductionism.** London, Hutchinson, 1967; New York, Macmillan, 1970.

A record of the Alpbach Symposium held in Switzerland in 1968 under Koestler's initiative. The rostrum of participants reads like a "who's who" of those in the scientific community who are concerned with the problem of the origin and nature of consciousness in man and his attendant aspirations. The entirely free exchanges which followed the reading of each paper are included, making the volume a reservoir of fresh, stimulating, and sometimes surprising ideas.

Koestler, Arthur. **The Ghost in the Machine.** London, Hutchinson, 1967; New York, Macmillan, 1968.

A stimulating volume by one who has established an international reputation as a highly informed layman who approaches the evidence for reductionism and finds it unsatisfactory. He demonstrates that the reductionist position is insufficient to account for the evidence in history of some serious flaw, some built-in deficiency, in the working of the human mind resulting from the explosive growth of the human brain. The book is a fresh approach to an old problem: the inability of man to diagnose his own nature correctly and order himself and society successfully.

Luria, A. R. **The Man With a Shattered World.** New York, Basic, 1972.

A book that is in a more popular style and may disappoint at times, but which does give a valuable insight into the world of a man who, as the result of a head wound, has virtually no short-term memory. So short is his memory span that even the beginning of a sentence may be forgotten before the end of it is reached. The record shows dramatically how important it is (and why) to have both a short-term and a long-term memory operating normally.

Penfield, Wilder. **The Mystery of the Mind.** Princeton: Princeton University Press; also, Toronto: Little, Brown & Co., 1975.

This is an overview of Penfield's research while treating epileptic patients in the Neurological Institute in Montreal. It is subtitled "A Critical Study of Consciousness and the Human Brain." Though the subject is often technical, Penfield's effective style, which is both pleasant and informative, easily manages the details of his pioneer work in this area. He describes how his findings led to some remarkable demonstrations of the primacy of the mind (or the "will") over the circuitry of the brain, showing that the mind appears quite capable of using the brain as a tool for its own purposes.

Popper, Sir Karl, and Eccles, Sir John. **The Self and Its Brain.** Springer Verlag International, 1977.

The subtitle is "An Argument for Interactionsim." This volume essentially takes the form of a debate between a philosopher of international repute and a neurophysiologist of similar stature, conducting an inquiry into the origin, nature, and even possible destiny of human consciousness. In considering these three fundamentally important subjects, differences of opinion do not in any way make the volume disjointed or contradictory. It is a large volume, both in size and reach, and makes what is perhaps a unique contribution to the current debate between those who see mindedness as a mere epiphenomenon of brain and those who see it as something of independent origin whose very nature suggests continuance even after the dissolution of the brain. There is, moreover, a real agreement between the two authors that the mind is master of the brain, making it its own. *The original title, "The Self and the Brain," was accordingly later reworded to read "The Self and* Its *Brain."*

Sherrington, Sir Charles. **Man on His Nature.** 2nd ed. Cambridge: Cambridge University Press, 1951.

This is the text of the Gifford Lectures presented by Sherrington in the University of Edinburgh during the winter of 1937-38. Revised and updated, it now represents the distilled wisdom of a prince among scientists contemplating the nature of the mind/brain relationship. It is written in retrospect of a lifetime spent in research, reflected upon by a man no longer concerned merely to preserve his reputation as orthodox and therefore entirely free to express some doubts as to the sufficiency of current reductionist views of the nature of man.

Papers

Best, J. Boyd. "Protopsychology." **Scientific American,** February 1963, pp. 55-62.

Kety, Seymour S. "A Biologist Examines the Mind and Behavior." **Science** 132 (1960): 1861-69.

Penfield, Wilder. "Engrams in the Human Brain." **Procedures of the Royal Society of Medicine** 61 (1968): 831-40.

———. "Epilepsy, Neurophysiology, and Some Brain Mechanisms Related to Consciousness" in **Basic Mechanisms of the Epilepsies.** Edited by H. H. Jasper, et al. Toronto: Little, Brown & Co., 1969.

——— and Perot, Phanor. "The Brain's Record of Auditory and Visual Experience—A Final Summary and Discussion." **Brain** 86 (1963): 595-696.

Notes

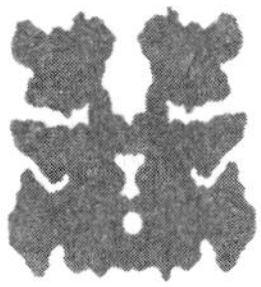

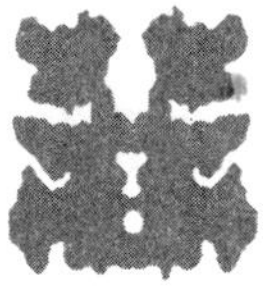